GHOSTS

By Henrik Ibsen

Adapted from William Archer's translation by
Alfred Enoch

sell a door
THEATRE COMPANY

www.selladoor.com

Published in 2013 by Sell A Door Theatre Company Ltd.
Athelney House, 161-165 Greenwich High Road, London, SE10 8JA
Tel: +44 (0) 20 3355 8567
E-mail: info@selladoor.com
www.selladoor.com

ISBN: 978-0-9574313-2-4

Cover image and design by deskTidy Design (www.desktidydesign.co.uk)

Visit www.selladoor.com to read more about our other publications and to
buy them. You will also find information on all our productions and how to
be involved. You can also sign up to our newsletter so that you can be kept
up to date with all our news and projects.

About Sell a Door Theatre Company Ltd.

Sell A Door Theatre Company was established in 2007 by a small group of artists studying at *The Liverpool Institute for Performing Arts* (www.lipa.ac.uk).

Sell A Door was incorporated in 2009 and since then has produced an impressive portfolio of work and has firmly established itself as a leading producer of mid-scale touring theatre. Sell a Door Theatre Company remains one of the few professional theatre companies producing this volume and quality of work with very little funding, and is reliant on its angels and investors to keep its work relevant and of a high quality.

Sell a Door Theatre Company aims to produce its season to cater for a wide genre of ages and tastes, yet the majority of its touring work is targeted at the young adult and teenage age bracket. Sell a Door Theatre Company faces a constant challenge of attracting young adults and teenagers (who usually would not attend live theatre) to see its shows and exciting them of the possibilities in theatre.

Sell A Door Theatre Company produced the debut UK Tour of *Spring Awakening,* the revival tour of *Lord of the Flies* to mark the centenary of William Golding and produced the first west end production of *Seussical* in the Christmas of 2012. *Spring Awakening* and *Lord of the Flies* established many new relationships between Sell A Door Theatre Company and dynamic regional theatres that share its values of producing exciting, relevant shows.

"As we continue to go from strength to strength it is thrilling to know that our audiences are coming along for the ride."

CAST

Mrs Alving	Deborah Blakc
Oswald Alving	Jason Langley
Pastor Manders	Robert Gill
Jacob Engstrand	Liam Smith
Regina Engstrand	Tamaryn Payne

CREATIVE TEAM

Producers	David Hutchinson & Phillip Rowntree
Adaptor	Alfred Enoch
Director	Anna Fox
Designer	Anna Lewis
Lighting Designer	Alexander Ridgers
Sound Designer	Tom Bartlett
Assistant Director	Joe Morrow
Vocal Coach	Pamela Dwyer
Graphic Design	DeskTidy Design

With special thanks to

James Corrigan, Alex Croft, Jack Faires, Suzie Preece, Amanda Reed, Chloë Wicks, English Touring Theatre & Makebelieve Arts

DEBORAH BLAKE (Mrs Alving)

Deborah covered the lead role of Maria Callas in Terence McNally's *Masterclass*, when it transferred from Broadway to the Vaudeville Theatre in the West End last year. Prior to this she evolved the comedic role of Lady Virginnia in Wilde's last attributed play, *Constance* (The Kings Head).

Other theatre includes: Comtesse de Saint Fond & Baronesse de Simiane (cover) *Madame de Sade* (Wyndham's Theatre for the Donmar West End Season), Martha (cover) *That Face* (Duke of York's), Catriona in *The Ride,* Betty Bell in *Mary Bell by Mary Bell* (White Bear), Oberon in *A Midsummer Night's Dream,* Isabella in *Measure for Measure,* Olivia in *Twelfth Night,* Queen in *Cymbeline* (The Original Shakespeare Company), Portia in *The Merchant of Venice* (Pentameters Theatre & Tour), Protoe in *Pentheselia* (The Gate Theatre), Miss Julie in *Miss Julie* (Northern Tour), Kissinda in *A Covent Garden Tragedy* (Tristan Bates Theatre), Sarah in *Another World* (Production Village), Mrs Marchmont/Mason in *An Ideal Husband* (Westminster Theatre & No.1National Tour), Mary in *The Mysteries* (The Orchard Theatre), Bella Manningham in *Gaslight* (Salon Varieties).

Television includes*: The Bill, Search, Secrets and Lies*

Film includes: *The Marlowe Report, Bad Science, Six Magic Numbers, Bare, Derive, The Omega Directive, Needles*

ROBERT GILL (Pastor Manders)

Theatre includes: Two national tours of *Calendar Girls, The Death of Norman Tortilla* (Tristan Bates Theatre), *The Years Between* (Royal Theatre, Northampton), *Someone Who'll Watch Over Me* (Barons Court Theatre), *Edward II* (Battersea Arts Centre), *Next Door's Baby* (Orange Tree Theatre), *Measure for Measure*, The Peter Hall Company (Bath/Stratford), *Habeas Corpus*, The Peter Hall Company (Bath/National Tour), *Mouth to Mouth* (Albery Theatre), *The Real Inspector Hound/Black Comedy* (Comedy Theatre, London/National Tour), *When We Are Married* (Savoy Theatre), *Don Juan* (Battersea Arts Centre), *Much Ado About Nothing* (Southwark Playhouse), *The Hired Man* (Haymarket

Theatre, Leicester & Astoria Theatre, London), *Grease* (National Tour), *Emma Bovary*, *Bedroom Farce* (Connaught Theatre, Worthing), *The Soldier's Tale* (Tour), *A Smashing Day* (Tour).

Film includes: *Hugo* (director: Martin Scorsese); *Oliver!*, *Chitty Chitty Bang Bang*.

Television includes: *Emmerdale* (Yorkshire Television), *Ocean of Fear* (Discovery Channel), *Silent Witness* (BBC), *A for Andromeda* (BBC), *Eastenders* (BBC).

Robert has just completed shooting the lead role in *Lose Control* a music video for *Hervè* directed by thirtytwo.

JASON LANGLEY (Oswald)

Jason trained at LAMDA after studying Drama at the University of Hull.

Theatre includes: *Nicked* (Hightide Festival), *ENRON* (West End & UK Tour), *PLAYlist* (Live Theatre Newcastle/Theatre 503), *Dick Whittington & His Cat* (Chipping Norton Theatre), *Sweet Charity* (Theatre Royal, Drury Lane).

Television includes: *Da Vinci's Demons* (BBC Worldwide/Starz), *World Without End* (Scott Free/Tandem), *Room At The Top* (BBC), *Doctors* (BBC), *The Bill* (ITV).

TAMARYN PAYNE (Regina)

Tamaryn trained at the Arts Educational School, graduating in 2010.

Theatre whilst in training includes: *As You Like It*, *Betrayal*, *Merchant of Venice*, *The Resistable Rise of Arturo Ui*.

Film and Television includes: *Hollyoaks* (Series Regular - Channel 4), *Vendetta* (Richwater Films).

LIAM SMITH (Engstrand)

Liam trained at Mountview Theatre School and Rose Bruford College.

Theatre includes: *Screaming in Advance* (The Wrestling School/Print Room), *Night Just Before The Forests* (Firehouse/Theatre 503), *Laburnum Grove* (Finborough), *Journey's End* (Sell A Door/Greenwich), *Henry V* (Theatre Delicatessen/Latitude), *12th Battle Of Isonzo* (Print Room), *Knives In Hens* (Theatre By The Lake), *Through The Night* (Finborough), *Hacked* (Theatre 503), *Blok/Eko* (Wrestling School/Exeter Northcott), *Judith: A Parting From The Body* (Cock Tavern), *Oliver Twisted, Robin Hood, Sleeping Beauty* (Portobello Panto/Tabernacle), *Prose & Cons* (Koestler Trust/Union Theatre), *Guns Or Butter, The Premature Burial, Terror* (Sticking Place), *All Men Are Whores* (Rosemary Branch), *Inherit The Wind* (Tricycle), *Dinner* (West End & National tour), *Song Of The Frogs* (Polka Theatre), *Urban Stories* (Theatre Lab), *The Golem, Charlotte Bronte* (Pascal Theatre), *Hatful Of Rain* (Wire), *The Rover, Woyzeck* (Bloomsbury/Theatre Box).

Film and Television includes: *Uncle* (Ch 4/Baby Cow), *Happiness* (Random Acts, Ch 4), *Hollyoaks* (Ch 4), *Locked Up Abroad* (National Geographic), *Sirens* (Daybreak/Ch 4), *End Of Love* (Partizan), *Roads* (Chapel Club), *Telstar* (Aspiration), *Cass* (Goldcrest), *Man For Hire* (HBO Europe), *Keep It Simple* (Talkback), *Holby City* (BBC).

ALFRED ENOCH (Adaptor)

Alfred studied Spanish and Portuguese Literature at Oxford University, where he adapted and directed Lope de Vega's *La Dama Boba*. *Ghosts* is his first professional writing credit.

He works primarily as an actor and his work in theatre includes: *Timon of Athens*, *Antigone* (National Theatre), *Happy New* (Old Red Lion), *Dinner* (Edinburgh Festival; Burton Taylor Studio), *The Seagull* (Oxford Playhouse).

Television includes: *Broadchurch* (Kudos/ITV), *The Mimic* [Pilot] (Running Bare/Ch 4).

Film: The *Harry Potter* series (Warner Bros.).

ANNA FOX (Director)

Anna is an Associate Director at Sell A Door Theatre Company.

Directing credits include: *Jessie Cave's Bookworm* (London/Edinburgh tour), *The History Boys* (Greenwich Theatre), *Dinner* (Edinburgh Festival; Burton Taylor Studio), *It Never Rains But it Pours* (Rosemary Branch Theatre), *Scene from a Cairo Classroom*, *Hostage Situation*, *Lips That Would Kiss* (Etcetera Theatre).

As creative associate: *Sincerely, Mr Toad* (UK Tour).

ANNA LEWIS (Designer)

Anna studied at Somerville College, Oxford.

Design credits include: *A Streetcar named Desire, The Seagull, The Picture of Dorian Gray, The Hothouse* (Oxford Playhouse), *Machinal, Dinner, Mojo* (National Tour), *Much Ado About Nothing* (International Tour - Produced by Thelma Holt).

Anna has recently been costume supervisor on a new adaption of *Miss Julie* by Reading Rep and has worked with the scenic art department of the Royal Opera House on their production of *Falstaff*.

ALEXANDER RIDGERS (Lighting Designer)

Alexander trained at the Royal Conservatoire of Scotland.

He has worked with National Youth Theatre, Tron Theatre, Tramway Theatre, and various other professional theatre companies around the UK. For Sell A Door Theatre Company, Alexander has designed *The History Boys, Hound of the Baskervilles, Rainbow, Peter, Seussical, Journey's End, Midsummer Nights Dream* and *1984*.

JOE MORROW (Assistant Director)

Joe graduated from the Italia Conti BA acting course in 2011.

Recent Productions: *RIP* (Musical Director/Composer), *News Revue* (Musical Director/Director), *Seussical* (Musical Director), *Aladdin*

(Musical Direction/Composer), *Spring Awakening* (Director), *They Shoot Horses, Don't They?* (Musical Director).

Joe is resident composer for *Such Stuff Theatre Company*, and is currently writing the music for their upcoming production *Mr Dream*.

He is also Associate Artistic Director for Waste of Space Theatre, the contemporary dance company based in Leeds and London, for whom he has directed the pieces *Terpsichorus Line, To Be or not To Beatles* and *Charging Through Marmite*.

DAVID HUTCHINSON (Producer)

David trained at the Liverpool Institute for Performing Arts and at the RSAMD. He also trained in writing at the Everyman Theatre, Liverpool.

Recent Directing and Producing credits include: *Journey's End* (Greenwich Theatre), *The Man Who Had All The Luck* (UK Tour), *Hound of the Baskervilles* (Greenwich Theatre), *Lord of the Flies* (UK Tour), *A Christmas Carol* (Greenwich Playhouse), *Proof* (Greenwich Playhouse), *Spring Awakening* (UK Tour), *Taste of Honey* (UK Tour), *The Comedy of Errors, Blue/Orange* (Greenwich Playhouse), *Dracula* (National Tour), *Six Ways The Musical* (Jermyn Street, London), *Falsettoland* (Edinburgh Fringe Festival 2009), *Planning Permission* (Unity Theatre, Liverpool).

PHILLIP ROWNTREE (Producer)

Phillip trained at the Liverpool Institute for Performing Arts as an Actor before becoming a Producer and Director.

Phillip has worked in the UK and throughout Europe and has directed shows such as *The History Boys* by Alan Bennett, *The Sugar Syndrome* by Lucy Prebble, *Treats* by Christopher Hampton and the first West End production of *Seussical* by Stephen Flaherty and Lynn Ahrens.

He is Managing Director of Sell a Door Theatre Company and has Co-Produced every production in its history. Phillip is also a Freelance Lecturer and Theatrical General Management Consultant.

A NOTE ON THE ADAPTATION

The basis of this adaptation of Ghosts is the 1890/1891 William Archer translation. In the introduction to Peter Watts' 1964 Penguin Classics edition of 'Ghosts and other plays' Watts praises Archer's translation, but writes: 'The trouble is that, naturally, he [Archer] translated the plays into the accepted theatrical language of his period,' which he blames for the 'ponderous stilted dialogue.'

Hoping to preserve what Watts calls 'felicities of translation that have never been bettered,' I have used Archer's translation as a starting point and, with reference to the Danish original, attempted to prepare a version of the text which is more easily intelligible and which sounds more natural to the modern ear. However, I have still endeavoured to keep the play firmly rooted in the period in which it was written; retaining a degree of linguistic formality and avoiding modern colloquialisms. The process will necessarily have modernised the text, however the intention is that this 'modernisation' does not stand out against the play's 19th century setting.

Archer's text faithfully reproduces Ibsen's rather prescriptive stage directions. As Ibsen wrote Ghosts in the knowledge that it was to be published and read before it was to be staged, these were clearly an important way of helping the reader visualize the action. However, it is my belief that in a production script these are far less useful. They might be of interest as a point of reference, but many of the choices they impose upon the actor may be made in rehearsal, where new possibilities may be explored. Therefore, I have eliminated a large number of the original stage directions from this adaptation.

Although I have not altered the period in which the play is set, I have translated the action from Western Norway to the Orkney Isles. The purpose of the new setting is to enable a level of specificity in production which I believe audiences have rightly come to expect of realist drama; allowing actors to adopt specific accents consistent with the setting of the play, and not as mere indicators of class.

To my mind Ghosts is a play of such strength and eloquence that it could speak to us of modern day British society even through the mouths of five 19th century Norwegians. But it is my hope that by bringing the action closer to home we will be further encouraged to examine the play's enduring relevance, and that by adjusting Archer's impressive translation for a modern audience, it will be easier to do so.

Alfred Enoch

Ghosts

This adaptation of GHOSTS was originally produced by David Hutchinson and Phillip Rowntree for *Sell A Door Theatre Company Ltd* at Greenwich Theatre, London on the 29th April 2013 with the following cast:

MRS ALVING, *widow to the late*   Deborah Blake
  Chamberlain Alving
OSWALD ALVING, *her son, a painter*   Jason Langley
PASTOR MANDERS, *a clergyman*   Robert Gill
JACOB ENGSTRAND, *a carpenter*   Liam Smith
REGINA ENGSTRAND, *Mrs Alving's maid* Tamaryn Payne

DIRECTOR   Anna Fox
DESIGNER   Anna Lewis
LIGHTING DESIGNER   Alexander Ridgers

The action takes place in Mrs Alving's house on the Orkney Isles.

ACT ONE.

A spacious garden-room, with one door to the left, and two doors to the right. In the middle of the room is a round table, with chairs about it. On the table lie books, periodicals, and newspapers. In the foreground to the left is a window, and by it a small sofa, with a worktable in front of it. In the background, the room is continued into a somewhat narrower conservatory, the walls of which are formed by large panes of glass. In the right-hand wall of the conservatory is a door leading down into the garden. Through the glass wall a gloomy Orcadian landscape is faintly visible, veiled by steady rain.

ENGSTRAND, the carpenter, stands by the garden door. His left leg is somewhat bent; he has a clump of wood under the sole of his boot. REGINA, with an empty garden syringe in her hand, hinders him from advancing.

REGINA. [*In a low voice*] What do you want? Stop right there; you're dripping wet!

ENGSTRAND. It's God's good rain, my girl.

REGINA. The devil's rain, more like.

ENGSTRAND. Lord, how you talk, Regina! Look, what I wanted to say—

REGINA. Don't go clattering about with that foot of yours! The young master's asleep upstairs.

ENGSTRAND. Asleep? In the middle of the day?

REGINA. That's no business of yours.

A beat.

ENGSTRAND. I was out on the loose last night—

REGINA. Oh, I can quite believe that.

ENGSTRAND. Yes, we're weak vessels, we poor mortals, my girl—

REGINA. So it seems.

ENGSTRAND. —and in this lowly world temptations abound. But all the same, I was hard at work, God knows, at half past five this morning!

REGINA. That's all very well, but won't you clear off! I don't want to be seen having a *rendez-vous* with you.

ENGSTRAND. What's that you say?

REGINA. I don't want to be found here with you; so just... get on about your business.

1

ENGSTRAND. Blest if I go before I've had a talk with you; I finish my work at the schoolhouse this afternoon, and then I'll be on to-night's boat and off home.

REGINA. Pleasant journey to you!

ENGSTRAND. Thank you, my child. You see, to-morrow the orphanage is to be opened, and there'll be revelry and high spirits, and plenty of intoxicating drink, you can be sure of that... And I shan't have anyone say that Jacob Engstrand can't keep out of temptations way!

REGINA. Oh?

ENGSTRAND. No! And certainly not when there's to be all sorts of fine folk here to-morrow. Pastor Manders is expected from town!

REGINA. He's coming to-day.

ENGSTRAND. There, you see! And you know, it would break my heart to give him cause to doubt me.

REGINA. Oho! is that your game?

ENGSTRAND. Is what my game?

REGINA. What are you trying to fool Pastor Manders into doing this time?

ENGSTRAND. Sh-sh! Are you crazy? Do I want to fool Pastor Manders? God no! Pastor Manders has been far too good a friend to me for that. But look, here's the point; I'm off home again to-night—

REGINA. The sooner the better, I say.

ENGSTRAND. Yes, but I want you with me, Regina.

REGINA. You want me—? What are you talking about?

ENGSTRAND. I want you to come home with me.

REGINA. You shall never get me to come home with you. Not in this life, at any rate.

ENGSTRAND. Oh, we'll see about that.

REGINA. Yes, you can be quite sure we'll 'see about it'! Me?! Who has been brought up by a lady like Mrs. Alving? Treated almost as a daughter here? You want me to go home with you?—and to a house like yours? For shame!

ENGSTRAND. What the devil do you mean? Do you dare set yourself up against your father, you hussy?

REGINA. You've often told me I was none of yours.

ENGSTRAND. Ah, don't worry yourself about that.

REGINA. Have you forgotten all the times you've sworn at me and called me a—? *Mon dieu*!

ENGSTRAND. Strike me down if I ever used as ugly a word as that.

REGINA. Oh, I remember very well the words you used.

ENGSTRAND. Yes, but that was only when I'd had a few, eh? For I'll tell you what, Regina, in this lowly world temptations do abound.

REGINA. Ugh!

ENGSTRAND. And besides, it was when your mother was having a go—I had to find something to get back at her with. Always had ideas above her station, that one. [*Mimics*.] "Let me go, Engstrand; let me be. Remember I was three years with Chamberlain Alving's family at Rosewood." [*Laughs*.] Lord have mercy! She could never forget the Captain was made a Chamberlain while she was in service here.

REGINA. Poor mother! You were the death of her.

ENGSTRAND. Oh, of course! I'm to blame for everything.

REGINA. Ugh—! And that leg!

ENGSTRAND. What was that, my child?

REGINA. *Pied de mouton.*

ENGSTRAND. That Latin, is it?

REGINA. Yes.

ENGSTRAND. Aye, aye, you've picked up some learning out here; and that may well come in useful now, Regina.

REGINA. What do you want with me in town?

ENGSTRAND. Can you have the heart to ask what a father wants with his only child? Aren't I a sad and lonely widower?

REGINA. Oh, don't try that one on me! Why do you want me?

ENGSTRAND. Well, let me tell you! I've been thinking of setting up in a new line of business.

REGINA. You've tried that often enough, for all the good it's done.

ENGSTRAND. Yes, but this time you'll see, Regina! Devil take me—

REGINA. Stop with your swearing!

ENGSTRAND. Hush, hush; you're right enough there, my girl. All I wanted to say was this; I've set aside a tidy sum from this Orphanage job—.

REGINA. Really? Well good for you.

ENGSTRAND. —but what can a man spend his ha'pence on out here in the middle of nowhere?

REGINA. Well, what then?

ENGSTRAND. Well, then, you see, I thought of investing that money. I thought a sort of a sailor's tavern—

REGINA. Ugh!

ENGSTRAND. A proper high-class affair, of course; not any old pig-sty for common sailors. No, damn it! It would be for captains and mates, and—and—you know, fancy folk.

REGINA. And you want me to—?

ENGSTRAND. To help, of course. Only for the look of the thing, you understand. You wouldn't have much to do in the way of work, my girl. You shall do exactly as you please.

REGINA. Shall I, indeed?

ENGSTRAND. But there must be a petticoat in the house; that's as clear as daylight. For I want to have it a bit lively like in the evenings, with singing and dancing, and so on. You mustn't forget they're weary wanderers on the ocean of life. Now don't be a fool and stand in your own light, Regina. What's to become of you out here? Your mistress has given you an education; but what good is that to you? You're to look after the children at the new Orphanage, I hear. Is that the sort of thing for you, eh? Are you so dead set on wearing your life out for a pack of dirty brats?

REGINA. No; if things go as I want them to... Well, there's no saying—there's no saying.

ENGSTRAND. What do you mean by that? "There's no saying"?

REGINA. Never you mind.—How much money have you saved?

ENGSTRAND. What with one thing and another, a matter of forty, forty-five pound.

REGINA. That's not so bad.

ENGSTRAND. Oh, it's enough to make a start with, my girl.

REGINA. Aren't you thinking of giving me any?

ENGSTRAND. No, I'm blest if I am!

REGINA. Not even of sending me a scrap of cloth for a new dress?

ENGSTRAND. Come to town with me, my lass, and you'll soon have dresses enough.

REGINA. [*Snorts derisively.*] I can do that on my own account, if I want to.

ENGSTRAND. No, a father's guiding hand is what you want, Regina. Now, I've got my eye on a lovely house in Little Harbour Street. They don't want much in the way of ready-money; and it could be a sort of a Sailors' Home, you know.

REGINA. But I will not live with you! And I don't want you interfering with my life, so clear off!

ENGSTRAND. You wouldn't stop long with me, my girl. No such luck! If you play your cards right, such a fine figure of a girl as you've grown into in the last year or two—

REGINA. Well?

ENGSTRAND. You'd soon get hold of some first mate—or maybe even a captain—

REGINA. I won't marry any one of that sort. Sailors have no *savoir vivre*.

ENGSTRAND. What was that?

REGINA. I tell you, I know what sailors are like. They're not the ones to marry.

ENGSTRAND. Then never mind about marrying them. You can make it pay all the same. He—the Norwegian—the man with the yacht—he paid sixty-five pound, he did; and she wasn't a bit handsomer than you.

REGINA. [*Making for him.*] GET OUT!

ENGSTRAND. [*Retreating.*] Now, now! You're not going to hit me, are you?

REGINA. Yes, if you talk about mother like that I shall hit you. Be off with you! [*Drives him back towards the garden door.*] And don't slam the door. Young Mr. Alving—

ENGSTRAND. Is asleep; I know. Ugh! You're mightily taken up with young Mr. Alving—Oho! you don't mean to say it's him you're—?

REGINA. Right, that's it; get out! You're crazy, I tell you! No, not that way; there comes Pastor Manders! Down the kitchen stairs.

ENGSTRAND. Yes, yes, I'm going. But just you have a word with him over there. He's the man to tell you what a child owes its father. For I am your father all the same, you know. I can prove it from the church register.

He goes out through the second door to the right, which REGINA opens and closes again after him. REGINA glances hastily at herself in the mirror, dusts herself with her pocket handkerchief and settles her necktie. Then she busies herself with the flowers.

PASTOR MANDERS, wearing an overcoat, carrying an umbrella, and with a small satchel on a strap over his shoulder, comes through the garden door into the conservatory.

MANDERS. Good-morning, Miss Engstrand.

REGINA. Oh! Good morning, Pastor Manders. Is the steamer in already?

MANDERS. It's just in. Terrible weather we've been having lately.

REGINA. It's very welcome out here in the country, sir.

5

MANDERS. Yes, of course; you're quite right. We townspeople give too little thought to that.

He begins to take off his overcoat.

REGINA. Oh, may I help you?—There! Why, look how wet it is! I'll just hang it up in the hall. And your umbrella, too—I'll open it so it has a chance to dry.

She goes out through the second door on the right with the overcoat and the umbrella. PASTOR MANDERS takes off his satchel and lays it and his hat on a chair. Meanwhile REGINA comes in again.

MANDERS. Ah, it's a relief to get out of the rain. I hope everything is going well up here?

REGINA. Yes, thank you, sir.

MANDERS. You have your hands full, I suppose, in preparation for to-morrow?

REGINA. Yes, there's plenty to do, of course.

MANDERS. And Mrs. Alving is at home, I trust?

REGINA. Oh, yes. She's just upstairs preparing the young master's chocolate.

MANDERS. Yes, tell me—I heard down at the pier that Oswald had arrived.

REGINA. That's right; he came the day before yesterday. We didn't expect him before to-day.

MANDERS. Fit and well, I hope?

REGINA. Yes, thank you, quite; but dreadfully tired from the journey. He came direct from Paris—I don't think he stopped over on the way. In fact, I think he's sleeping a little now, so perhaps we'd better talk a little quietly.

MANDERS. Sh!—as quietly as you please.

REGINA. Do sit down, Pastor Manders; make yourself comfortable.

He sits down; she places a footstool under his feet.

There we are. How's that, sir?

MANDERS. Thank you, thank you; that's wonderful.

A beat.

Do you know, Miss Engstrand, I am of the opinion that you've grown since I last saw you.

REGINA. Do you think so, Sir? Mrs. Alving says I've filled out too.

MANDERS. Filled out? Well, perhaps a little; just enough.

Short pause.

6

REGINA. Shall I tell Mrs. Alving you're here?

MANDERS. Oh, no, there's no hurry, my dear child. But thank you.—Ah! by-the-bye: Regina, my dear girl, you must tell me: how is your father getting on out here?

REGINA. Oh, he's getting on well enough, thank you, sir.

MANDERS. He called on me last time he was in town.

REGINA. Did he really? He's always so glad of a chance to talk to you, sir.

MANDERS. And you often look in on him at his work, I daresay?

REGINA. I—? Oh, of course, when I have time, I—

MANDERS. Your father is not a man of strong character, Miss Engstrand. He stands terribly in need of a guiding hand.

REGINA. Oh, yes; I daresay he does.

MANDERS. He requires some one near him whom he cares for, and whose judgment he respects. He frankly admitted as much when he last came to see me.

REGINA. Yes, he mentioned something of the sort to me. But I don't know whether Mrs. Alving can spare me; especially now that we've got the new Orphanage to attend to. And I should be very sorry to leave Mrs. Alving; she has always been so kind to me.

MANDERS. But a daughter's duty, my good girl!—Of course, we should first have to get your mistress's consent.

REGINA. But I'm not sure whether it would be quite proper for me, at my age, to keep house for a single man.

MANDERS. What! My dear Miss Engstrand! When the man is your own father?

REGINA. Yes, that may be; but all the same—Now, if it were in a respectable home, and with a real gentleman—

MANDERS. Why, my dear Regina—

REGINA.—one I could love and respect, and be a daughter to—

MANDERS. Yes, but my dear child—

REGINA. Then I might even be glad to go to town. It's very lonely out here. You know yourself, sir, what it is to be alone in the world. And I can assure you I'm both quick and willing. Don't you know of any such place for me, sir?

MANDERS. I? No, certainly not.

REGINA. But, dear, kind Sir, do remember me if—

MANDERS. [Rising.] Yes, yes, certainly, Miss Engstrand.

REGINA. For if I—

MANDERS. Will you be so good as to tell your mistress I am here?

REGINA. Yes, sir; right away.

She goes out to the left. PASTOR MANDERS paces the room two or three times, stands a moment in the background with his hands behind his back, and looks out over the garden. Then he returns to the table, picks up a book, and looks at the title-page. He starts, and then proceeds to looks at rest of the books on the table.

MANDERS. Good heavens!

The door on the left opens and MRS. ALVING enters; she is followed by REGINA, who immediately goes out by the first door on the right.

MRS. ALVING. Welcome, my dear Pastor.

MANDERS. How do you do, Mrs. Alving? Here I am, as promised.

MRS. ALVING. And as punctual as ever.

MANDERS. You mustn't mind if I tell you it wasn't so easy for me to get away. What with all the Boards and Committees I belong to—

MRS. ALVING. Which makes it all the kinder of you to come so early. Now we can get through our business before lunch. But where's your bag?

MANDERS. I left it down at the inn. I shall sleep there to-night.

MRS. ALVING. [*Suppressing a smile.*] You really can't be persuaded to pass the night under my roof? Even now?

MANDERS. No, no, Mrs. Alving; many thanks. I shall stay at the inn, as usual. It's very near the pier; most convenient.

MRS. ALVING. Well, you must have your own way. But I really should have thought that two elderly people like us—

MANDERS. Now you are making fun of me. Well, naturally you're in great spirits to-day—what with to-morrow's celebrations and Oswald's return.

MRS. ALVING. Yes, it's a joy to have him back! It's more than two years since he was home last. And now he's promised to stay with me all winter.

MANDERS. Has he really? How dutiful of him! For I can well believe that life in Rome and Paris has very different attractions from any we can offer here.

MRS. ALVING. Ah, but here he has his mother, you see. That's my darling boy—he hasn't forgotten his old mother!

MANDERS. It would be grievous indeed, if absence and absorption in art and that sort of thing were to blunt his natural feelings.

MRS. ALVING. Yes, it would. But there's nothing of that sort to fear with him. I'm quite curious to see whether you'll recognize him. He'll be down presently; he's just upstairs now, resting a little on the sofa. But do sit down, my dear Pastor.

MANDERS. Thank you. Are you quite at liberty to—?

MRS. ALVING. Certainly.

She sits by the table.

MANDERS. Very well. Then let me show you these...

He goes to the chair where his satchel lies, takes out a packet of papers, then sits down on the opposite side of the table, and tries to clear a space for the papers.

Now, to begin with, here is—[*Breaking off.*] Tell me, Mrs. Alving, how do these books come to be here?

MRS. ALVING. These? I'm reading them.

MANDERS. Do you read this sort of literature?

MRS. ALVING. Certainly.

MANDERS. Do you feel better or happier for such reading?

MRS. ALVING. I feel, in a sense, more secure.

MANDERS. What on earth can you mean?

MRS. ALVING. Well, I seem to find explanation and confirmation of all sorts of things I myself have been thinking. And that's the truly amazing thing, Pastor Manders; there really is nothing new in these books, nothing that most people don't think already. Only most people either don't engage with these thoughts, or else they keep quiet about it.

MANDERS. Good God! Do you really believe that most people—?

MRS. ALVING. Yes, I do.

MANDERS. But surely not in this country? Not here amongst us?

MRS. ALVING. Why not? Here's no different to anywhere else.

MANDERS. Well, really, I must say—!

MRS. ALVING. But what exactly is it that you object to in these books?

MANDERS. Exactly!? What exactl—? Mrs. Alving, you surely don't suppose that I have nothing better to do than study publications such as these?

MRS. ALVING. So you know nothing of what you're condemning.

MANDERS. I have read enough about these writings to disapprove of them.

MRS. ALVING. Yes; but your own judgment—

MANDERS. My dear Mrs. Alving, there are many occasions in life when one must rely upon the judgements of others. That is the way of the world! And it is just as well; else what would become of society?

MRS. ALVING. Yes, well, I suppose you're right there.

MANDERS. Besides, I of course do not deny that there may be much that is attractive in such books. Nor can I blame you for wishing to keep up with the intellectual movements that are said to be going on in the great world; after all, that is where you have let your son pass so much of his life. But—

MRS. ALVING. But?

MANDERS. [*Lowering his voice.*] But one should not talk about it, Mrs. Alving. One is certainly not bound to account to everybody for what one reads and thinks within one's own four walls.

MRS. ALVING. Of course not; I quite agree with you.

MANDERS. And, naturally, you must consider the interests of this Orphanage, which you decided on founding at a time when—if I understand you rightly—you thought very differently on spiritual matters.

MRS. ALVING. Oh, yes; I quite admit that. But it was about the Orphanage—

MANDERS. It was about the Orphanage that we were going to speak; yes. All I say is: prudence, my dear lady! And now let us get down to business.

He opens the packet, and takes out a number of papers.

Do you see these?

MRS. ALVING. The documents?

MANDERS. Every last one—and in perfect order. I can tell you it was no mean feat to get them in time. I had to apply a certain degree of pressure. The authorities are almost morbidly scrupulous when there is any decisive step to be taken, but here they are at last. See here; this is the formal deed of gift of the parcel of land known as Sunhill in the Manor of Rosewood, with all the newly constructed buildings, schoolrooms, master's house, and chapel. And here is the writ for the endowment and for the Bye-laws of the Institution. Would you care to have a read? [*Reads.*] "Bye-laws for the Children's Home to be known as 'Captain Alving's Foundation'"

MRS. ALVING. [*After a long look at the paper.*] So there it is.

MANDERS. I decided on 'Captain' rather than 'Chamberlain'. 'Captain' looks less pretentious.

MRS. ALVING. Oh, yes; whatever you think best.

MANDERS. And here you have the bank account of the capital lying at interest to cover the expenses of the Orphanage.

MRS. ALVING. Thank you; but would you keep it—it would be more convenient.

MANDERS. With pleasure. I think we will leave the money in the Bank for the present. Although the interest is certainly not what we could wish: four per cent, and six months' notice of withdrawal. If a good mortgage could be found later on—of course it must be of unimpeachable security—then we could perhaps reconsider.

MRS. ALVING. Certainly, my dear Pastor. You are the best judge in these matters.

MANDERS. I will keep my eyes open at any rate.—But there is another matter that I've been meaning to ask you about.

MRS. ALVING. And what is that?

MANDERS. Shall the Orphanage be insured or not?

MRS. ALVING. Of course it must be insured.

MANDERS. Well, just a moment, Mrs. Alving. Let us look into the matter a little more closely.

MRS. ALVING. I have everything insured; buildings, movables, stock, crops—everything.

MANDERS. Of course you do—on your own estate. And so have I—naturally. But here, you see, it is quite another matter. The Orphanage is to be... consecrated, as it were, to a higher purpose.

MRS. ALVING. Yes, but that's no reason—

MANDERS. For my own part, I should certainly not see the slightest impropriety in guarding against all eventualities.

MRS. ALVING. No, I should think not.

MANDERS. But what is the general feeling in the neighbourhood? You, of course, will know better than I.

MRS. ALVING. Well... the general feeling—

MANDERS. Is there any considerable number of people—significant people, you understand—who might be scandalised?

MRS. ALVING. What do you mean by 'significant people'?

MANDERS. Well, I mean people in such important and influential positions that one cannot help attaching some weight to their opinions.

MRS. ALVING. There are several people of that sort here, who, most likely, would be very shocked if—

MANDERS. There, you see! In town we too have many such people. Think of all my colleagues' followers! People would be only too ready to interpret our action as a sign that neither you nor I had faith in Divine Providence.

MRS. ALVING. But my dear Pastor, at the very least you can assure yourself that—

MANDERS. Yes, I know—I know; my conscience would be quite easy, that is true enough. But nevertheless we should not escape grave misinterpretation; and that might very likely reflect unfavourably upon the Orphanage.

MRS. ALVING. Well, in that case—

MANDERS. Nor can I entirely lose sight of the difficult—I might even say painful—position in which I might perhaps find myself. In the leading circles of the town, people take a lively interest in this Orphanage. It is, of course, founded partly for the benefit of the town, as well; and it is hoped that it will result in a significant improvement in our Poor Rates. Now, as I have been your adviser, and have had the business arrangements in my hands, I cannot but fear that I may have to bear the brunt of this fanaticism—

MRS. ALVING. Well, you mustn't risk that.

MANDERS. Not to mention the attacks that would undoubtedly be made upon me in certain papers and periodicals, which—

MRS. ALVING. Enough, my dear Pastor! That consideration is quite decisive.

MANDERS. Then you do not wish the Orphanage to be insured?

MRS. ALVING. No. We will let it alone.

MANDERS. But if a disaster were to occur? One can never be sure— Would you be able to make good the damage?

MRS. ALVING. No; I must tell you plainly, I wouldn't.

MANDERS. Then I must tell you, Mrs. Alving—we are taking no small responsibility upon ourselves.

MRS. ALVING. Do you think we can do otherwise?

MANDERS. No, and there's the rub; we really cannot do otherwise. We ought not to expose ourselves to misinterpretation, and we certainly mustn't offend the faithful.

MRS. ALVING. You, as a clergyman, certainly mustn't.

MANDERS. And I truly believe that we may trust that such an institution has fortune on its side; that it does, in fact, stand under a special providence.

MRS. ALVING. Let us hope so, Pastor Manders.

MANDERS. Then shall we leave matters as they are?

MRS. ALVING. Yes, certainly.

MANDERS. Very well. So be it. [*Makes a note.*] —No insurance.

MRS. ALVING. It's odd that you should happen to mention this to-day—

MANDERS. I have long been meaning to ask you of it.

MRS. ALVING.—for we very nearly had a fire down there yesterday.

MANDERS. You don't say!

MRS. ALVING. Oh, it was nothing. A heap of shavings caught fire in the carpenter's workshop.

MANDERS. Where Engstrand works?

MRS. ALVING. Yes. They say he's often careless with matches.

MANDERS. He has so much on his mind, that man—so many temptations. At least I've heard he is now striving to lead a decent life, thank God.

MRS. ALVING. Is he really? And where did you hear that?

MANDERS. He told me so himself.

MRS. ALVING. Ha!

MANDERS. And he is certainly an excellent workman.

MRS. ALVING. Oh, yes; so long as he's sober...

MANDERS. Well, yes, it's a wretched vice, but he says it's his poor leg that drives him to it. Last time he was in town I was very touched by him. He came and thanked me most warmly for having got him work here, for it allowed him to be near Regina.

MRS. ALVING. He doesn't see much of her.

MANDERS. Certainly; he told me he talks to her every day.

MRS. ALVING. Well, perhaps.

MANDERS. He feels so acutely that he needs someone to keep a firm hold on him when temptation comes. That is what I cannot help liking about Jacob Engstrand: he comes to you so full of contrition and self-reproach; so helpless! The last time I spoke with him... Mrs. Alving, if it were a real necessity for him to have Regina home again—

MRS. ALVING. Regina!?

MANDERS.—you must not set yourself against it.

MRS. ALVING. Indeed I shall set myself against it. And besides, Regina is to have a position in the Orphanage.

MANDERS. But nevertheless, you must remember he is her father.

MRS. ALVING. Oh, I know very well what sort of a father he's been to her. No! She shall never go to Engstrand; not with my blessing.

MANDERS. My dear lady, you mustn't get so excited. You sadly misjudge poor Engstrand. You seem to be quite terrified—

MRS. ALVING. I'm afraid my mind is made up. I have taken Regina into my house, and there she shall stay. [*Stopping PASTOR MANDERS in his tracks.*] Hush, my dear Pastor Manders; say no more about it. Listen! That'll be Oswald coming downstairs. Now we'll think of no one but him.

OSWALD ALVING, in a light overcoat, hat in hand, and smoking a large meerschaum pipe, enters by the door on the left; he stops in the doorway.

OSWALD. Oh, I beg your pardon; I thought you were in the study. Good-morning, Pastor Manders.

MANDERS. Well, I never!

MRS. ALVING. What do you make of him, Pastor?

MANDERS. I, er...—can it really be—?

OSWALD. The Prodigal Son? Indeed so, sir.

MANDERS. [*Protesting.*] Oh, my dear boy—

OSWALD. Well then, the Lost Sheep returned to the fold.

MRS. ALVING. Oswald is thinking of the time when you were so much opposed to his becoming a painter.

MANDERS. To our human eyes many a step seems dubious, which afterwards proves—[*Wrings his hand.*] But first of all, welcome, welcome home! You mustn't think, my dear Oswald—I suppose I may call you by your Christian name?

OSWALD. What else should you call me?

MANDERS. Very well. But what I wanted to say was this: you must not think that I utterly condemn the artist's calling. I have no doubt there are many who can keep their inner selves unharmed in that profession, as in any other.

OSWALD. Let us hope so.

MRS. ALVING. [*Beaming with delight.*] I know one who has kept both his inner and his outer self unharmed. Just look at him, Pastor Manders.

OSWALD. Yes, yes, mother; let's say no more about it.

MANDERS. Why, certainly—that is undeniable. And you have begun to make a name for yourself already. The newspapers have often mentioned you, and most favourably. Although lately I don't seem to have seen your name quite so often...

OSWALD. [*From the conservatory.*] I haven't been able to paint so much lately.

MRS. ALVING. Even a painter needs a little rest now and then.

MANDERS. Oh, I can imagine. He must regain his strength so he can rouse himself for some great work.

OSWALD. Yes.—Mother, will lunch be ready soon?

MRS. ALVING. In less than half an hour. He has a tremendous appetite, thank God.

MANDERS. And a taste for tobacco, too, I see.

OSWALD. I found my father's pipe in my room.

MANDERS. Ah!—then that accounts for it!

MRS. ALVING. For what?

MANDERS. When Oswald appeared in the doorway, with the pipe in his mouth, it was as if I'd seen his father.

OSWALD. No, really?

MRS. ALVING. Oh, how can you say that! Oswald takes after me.

MANDERS. Yes, but there is something about the corners of his mouth—something about the lips—that reminds me exactly of Alving: or at least, now that he's smoking it does.

MRS. ALVING. Nonsense. I think Oswald has rather a clerical curve to his mouth.

MANDERS. Oh yes, yes; some of my colleagues have much the same expression.

MRS. ALVING. But do put your pipe away, my dear boy; I won't have smoking in here.

OSWALD. [*He does so.*] By all means. I only tried it because I remembered smoking it once as a child.

MRS. ALVING. Really?

OSWALD. Yes. I was quite small at the time. I remember I went up to father's room one evening when he was in great spirits.

MRS. ALVING. Oh, surely you can't remember anything of those times.

OSWALD. Oh yes; distinctly! He took me on his knee, and gave me the pipe. "Smoke, boy," he said; "smoke away!" And I smoked as hard as I could, until I felt myself growing quite pale and large beads of sweat forming on my forehead. Then he burst out laughing—

MANDERS. How strange.

MRS. ALVING. My dear friend, it's only something Oswald has dreamt.

OSWALD. No, mother, I can assure you I didn't dream it; for you came and carried me out to the nursery—don't you remember? And I was sick, and you started crying.—Did father often play such practical jokes?

MANDERS. In his youth he overflowed with the joy of life.

15

OSWALD. And yet he managed to do so much in the world; so much that was good and useful; even though he died so early.

MANDERS. Yes, you have inherited the name of an energetic and admirable man, my dear Oswald Alving. No doubt it will be an incentive to you.

OSWALD. It certainly ought to be.

MANDERS. It was very good of you to come home for the ceremony.

OSWALD. I could do no less for my father.

MRS. ALVING. And I shall get to keep him for so long! That's the best part of it.

MANDERS. You're going to pass the winter at home, I hear.

OSWALD. My stay is indefinite, Pastor. But it is good to be home!

MRS. ALVING. Oh, it is, isn't it, dear?

MANDERS. [*With sympathy.*] You went out into the world early, my dear Oswald.

OSWALD. I did. I sometimes wonder whether it wasn't too early.

MRS. ALVING. Oh no, not at all. A healthy boy is all the better for it; especially when he's an only child. He oughtn't to hang about at home with his mother and father, and get spoilt.

MANDERS. That is a very disputable point, Mrs. Alving. A child's proper place is, and always will be, his father's house.

OSWALD. There I quite agree with you, Pastor Manders.

MANDERS. Take your son, for example—there's no reason why we should not say it in his presence—what has the consequence been for him? He is twenty-six or twenty-seven, and he has never had the opportunity of learning what a decent home really is.

OSWALD. I beg your pardon, Pastor, but there you're quite mistaken.

MANDERS. Indeed? I thought you had lived almost exclusively in artistic circles.

OSWALD. So I have.

MANDERS. And chiefly among the younger artists?

OSWALD. Absolutely.

MANDERS. But I thought few of those young fellows could afford to set up house and support a family.

OSWALD. There are many who cannot afford to marry, sir.

MANDERS. Well, there we are.

OSWALD. But, none the less, they may still have a home. And several of them do, in fact; and very pleasant, decent homes they are, too.

16

MRS. ALVING follows the exchange with breathless interest. She nods, but says nothing.

MANDERS. But I'm not talking of bachelors' quarters. By a home I understand the home of a family, where a man lives with his wife and children.

OSWALD. Yes; or with his children and his children's mother.

MANDERS. But, good heavens—!

OSWALD. Well?

MANDERS. Lives with—his children's mother!

OSWALD. Yes. Would you have him turn her out of doors?

MANDERS. Then these are illicit relations you are referring to! Irregular marriages, as people call them!

OSWALD. I have never noticed anything particularly irregular about the lives these people lead.

MANDERS. But how is it possible that a—a young man or young woman with any decency of feeling can endure to live like that?—and in the eyes of all the world!

OSWALD. What else can they do? A poor young artist—a poor girl—marriage costs a great deal, Pastor Manders.

MANDERS. What else can they do? Please let me tell you, Mr. Alving, what else they 'can' do. They 'can'—and ought!—to exercise self-restraint from the first; that is what they 'can' do.

OSWALD. That approach wouldn't find much favour among young people who love each other.

MRS. ALVING. It certainly wouldn't!

MANDERS. [*Continuing.*] How can the authorities tolerate such things? Allow them to carry on openly like that!? [*Confronting MRS. ALVING.*] Had I not cause to be deeply concerned about your son? In circles where open immorality is rife!—celebrated, even!

OSWALD. I shall let you in on a little secret, Pastor. In Paris I would spend most of my Sundays in such 'irregular' homes—

MANDERS. Sunday of all days!

OSWALD. The day of rest. Surely that's the day to enjoy one's self? Well, anyway, never have I heard an offensive word, and still less witnessed anything that could be called immoral. But do you know when and where I have come across immorality in artistic circles?

MANDERS. No, and I thank God that I don't!

OSWALD. Well, then, you must forgive me for telling you. I have only encountered it when some of our very own 'decent' husbands and fathers

17

have come to Paris and done us poor artists the honour of visiting our humble abodes. And what an education they were able to give us! These gentlemen could certainly tell us a thing or two of 'the ways of the world'.

MANDERS. What! Do you mean to say that respectable men—from this country—?

OSWALD. Have you never heard these respectable men, when they get home again, talking about the way in which immorality runs rampant abroad?

MANDERS. Yes, many times—

MRS. ALVING. As have I.

OSWALD. Well, you may take their word for it; they know what they're talking about! —Arrgh! I can't stand hearing those great, glorious, free lives they lead over there defamed like that!

MRS. ALVING. You mustn't get worked up, Oswald. It's not good for you.

OSWALD. Yes; you're quite right, mother. It's bad for me, I know. You see, I'm wretchedly worn out. I shall go for a little stroll before lunch. Forgive me, Pastor: I know you can't accept my point of view but I couldn't help speaking out.

He goes out by the second door to the right.

MRS. ALVING. My poor boy!

MANDERS. You may well say so. Then this is what has become of him!

There is a silence. PASTOR MANDERS walks back and forth and MRS. ALVING glowers at him.

He called himself the Prodigal Son. Dreadful... dreadful!

The silence persists. MRS. ALVING continues to glower at PASTOR MANDERS who continues to pace as before.

And what do you say to all this?

MRS. ALVING. I say that Oswald was right in every word.

MANDERS. Right? Right! In such principles?

MRS. ALVING. Here, in my loneliness, I have come to the same way of thinking, Pastor Manders. But I have never dared to say anything. Well, now my son shall speak for me.

MANDERS. You are greatly to be pitied, Mrs. Alving. But now I must speak seriously to you. And it is no longer as your business manager and advisor that I stand before you, nor as an old friend to you and to your husband. It is as a priest—the very priest who stood before you at your life's most desperate moment.

MRS. ALVING. And what has the priest to say to me?

MANDERS. I will first stir up your memory a little; the time is apt. To-morrow will be the tenth anniversary of your husband's death. To-morrow the memorial in his honour will be unveiled. And to-morrow I shall have to speak to the whole assembled multitude. But to-day I will speak to you alone.

MRS. ALVING. Very well, Pastor Manders. Speak.

MANDERS. Do you remember that after less than a year of married life you stood on the verge of an abyss? You forsook your house and home, fled from your husband—Yes, Mrs. Alving, fled. Fled, and refused to return to him, however much he begged and prayed.

MRS. ALVING. Have you forgotten how infinitely miserable I was in that first year?

MANDERS. It is the very mark of the spirit of rebellion to crave for happiness in this life. What right have we human beings to happiness? We have simply to do our duty, Mrs. Alving! And your duty was to hold firmly to the man you had once chosen, and to whom you were bound by the holiest ties.

MRS. ALVING. You know very well what sort of life Alving was leading—the excesses he was guilty of.

MANDERS. I know the rumours that were circulating about him; and I would be the last to approve the life he led in his former days, if these were, in fact, correct. But a wife is not appointed to be her husband's judge. It was your duty to bear with humility the cross which a Higher Power had, in its wisdom, laid upon you. But instead, you cast off the cross, deserting the poor sinner whom you should have supported, and go and risk your good name and reputation—not to mention those of other people.

MRS. ALVING. Other people? I think you mean one other person's.

MANDERS. It was incredibly reckless of you to seek refuge with me.

MRS. ALVING. With our priest? Our intimate friend?

MANDERS. Precisely for that reason. You may thank God that I possessed the necessary strength of character to dissuade you from your wild designs; and that it fell to me to lead you back to the path of duty, and home to your lawful husband.

MRS. ALVING. Well, Pastor Manders, that was certainly your doing.

MANDERS. I was but a poor instrument in a Higher Plan. And has it not proved a blessing to you, all the days of your life, that I induced you once more to take up the yoke of duty and obedience? Did not everything happen as I foretold? Alving renounced his sins, as good men do, and showed himself an exemplary husband for the rest of his days. Why, he even became a benefactor to the whole region, and made you his assistant so that you might share in his achievements. And a wonderful assistant you were, too—oh, I know, Mrs. Alving; that praise is due to you.—But now I come to the next great error in your life.

MRS. ALVING. And what is that?

MANDERS. Just as you once refused the duty of a wife, so have you since the duty of a mother.

MRS. ALVING. Ah—!

MANDERS. All your life you have been under the dominion of a wicked and impulsive wilfulness, and, as a result, you have developed an extraordinary propensity for lawlessness and insubordination. You have never known how to endure any bond; everything that has weighed upon you in life you have discarded without care or conscience, like a burden you were free to throw off at will. It did not please you to be a wife any longer, so you left your husband. And when you found it troublesome to be a mother, you sent your child away to be brought up by strangers.

MRS. ALVING. Yes, that is true. I did do that.

MANDERS. And as a result you have become a stranger to him.

MRS. ALVING. No! No, that I'm not.

MANDERS. Of course you are; you must be! And in what state of a mind has he returned to you? Listen to me, Mrs. Alving, and listen well. You sinned greatly against your husband; that you recognise by raising a memorial to him. Recognise now, also, how you have sinned against your son—there may yet be time to lead him back from the path of the wicked. Turn back yourself, and save what may yet be saved in him. For truly, Mrs. Alving, you have failed in your duty as a mother! This I have thought it my duty to tell you.

Silence.

MRS. ALVING. [*Slowly and with self-control.*] Now you have spoken, Pastor Manders; and to-morrow you shall speak publicly in memory of my husband. I shall not speak to-morrow, but now I shall, and frankly. As you have spoken to me.

MANDERS. No doubt you will attempt to excuse yourself—

MRS. ALVING. I shall do nothing of the sort.

MANDERS. Well—?

MRS. ALVING. All that you have just said about me and my husband—about our life after you had brought me back to 'the path of duty', as you called it—all that, you know nothing of from personal observation. From that moment you, who had been our intimate friend, never set foot in our house again.

MANDERS. You and your husband left the town immediately after.

MRS. ALVING. Yes; and in my husband's lifetime you never once came to see us. It was business that finally forced you to visit me when you undertook the affairs of the Orphanage.

MANDERS. [*Softly.*] Helen—if that is meant as a reproach, I would beg you to bear in mind—

MRS. ALVING.—the regard you owed to your position, yes; and I was a runaway wife. One can never be too cautious with a fallen woman.

MANDERS. My dear Hel...—Mrs. Alving, you know that is an absurd exaggeration—

MRS. ALVING. Yes, I'm sure it is. My point is that your judgment of my married life is founded upon nothing but hearsay.

MANDERS. I don't deny it. What then?

MRS. ALVING. Then, Pastor Manders, you must hear the truth. I have sworn to myself that one day you should know it—you and you alone.

MANDERS. Well, what is it?

MRS. ALVING. The truth is that my husband died just as dissolute as he had lived.

MANDERS. What did you say!?

MRS. ALVING. After nineteen years of marriage, as dissolute—in his desires at any rate—as he was before you married us.

MANDERS. And those—those indiscretions—those irregularities—excesses, if you like—you call those 'a dissolute life'?

MRS. ALVING. It was our doctor who used the expression.

MANDERS. Your doctor!? I don't understand you.

MRS. ALVING. You need not.

MANDERS. It's enough to make your head reel. Your whole married life, the seeming union of all those years, was nothing more than a sham?

MRS. ALVING. Precisely. Now you know.

MANDERS. This is—this is inconceivable to me. I cannot comprehend it! I cannot believe it! How is it possible that—? How could something like that be kept secret?

MRS. ALVING. That has been my life's work. After Oswald was born, I thought Alving seemed to be a little better. But it did not last long. And then I had to struggle twice as hard, fighting for my life, so that nobody should know what sort of man my child's father was. And you know how likeable Alving was. Nobody seemed able to believe anything but good of him. He was one of those men whose lives cannot dent their reputation. But then, Pastor—for you must know the whole story—the most appalling thing of all happened.

MANDERS. More appalling than what you have told me already?

MRS. ALVING. I had gone on bearing with him, although I knew very well the sordid secrets of his private life. But when he brought the scandal within our own walls—

MANDERS. Impossible! Here!?

MRS. ALVING. Yes; here in our own home. It was there, in the dining-room, that I first came to know of it. I was busy with something in there, and the door was standing ajar. I heard our housemaid come up from the garden, with water for the flowers.

MANDERS. Well—?

MRS. ALVING. Soon after, I heard Alving come in too. I heard him say something softly to her. And then I heard—[*With a short laugh*]—oh! it still sounds in my ears, so hateful and yet so ludicrous—I heard my own maidservant whisper, "Let me go, Mr. Alving! Let me be!"

MANDERS. That was unseemly levity on his part, but it cannot have been more than that, Mrs. Alving; believe me, it cannot.

MRS. ALVING. I soon knew what to believe. Mr. Alving had his way with the girl; and that connection had consequences, Pastor Manders.

MANDERS. Such things in this house—in this house!

MRS. ALVING. I have borne a great deal in this house. To keep him at home in the evenings, and at night, I had to join him as he drunk himself into a stupor up in his room. I would have to sit there; clinking glasses and drinking with him, listening to his idiotic, vulgar talk. I have had to fight with him to get him dragged to bed—

MANDERS. And you were able to bear all this!

MRS. ALVING. I had to bear it for my little boy's sake. But when this last insult was added; when my own maidservant—; then I swore to myself: No more! And so I took matters in to my own hands; took control. Of him, the house... everything. For now I had a weapon against him, you see; he dared not oppose me. It was then I sent Oswald away from home. He was nearly seven years old, and was beginning to observe and ask questions, as children do. That I could not bear. It seemed to me he'd be infected by merely breathing the air of this polluted house. That was why I sent him away. And now you can also see why he was never allowed to set foot inside this house so long as his father lived. No one knows what that cost me.

MANDERS. So you have indeed had a life of trial.

MRS. ALVING. I could never have borne it had it not been for my work. For I can truly say that I have worked! All the additions to the estate, all the improvements—the machinery that Alving was so much praised for having introduced—do you suppose he had the energy for anything of the sort? He would lie all day on the sofa, reading an old Court Guide! Even when he did have his better intervals, it was I who urged him on; just as it was I who had to do everything when he relapsed into his evil ways, or else incapacitated himself with his own tremendous self-pity.

MANDERS. And it is to this man that you raise a memorial?

MRS. ALVING. Such is the power of a guilty conscience.

MANDERS. A guilty conscience? What do you mean?

MRS. ALVING. It always seemed inevitable to me that one day the truth would come out. So I built the Orphanage to deaden all rumours and resolve any doubts.

MANDERS. Well, in that you have surely succeeded, Mrs. Alving.

MRS. ALVING. I had another reason, apart from that. I was determined that Oswald should inherit nothing whatsoever from his father.

MANDERS. Then it is Alving's fortune that—?

MRS. ALVING. Yes. Everything that I have spent on the Orphanage, year after year, totals the exact amount—and I have calculated it precisely— the exact amount that made Lieutenant Alving 'a good match' in his day.

MANDERS. I don't understand why—

MRS. ALVING. They say everything has a price, and that, it seems, was mine. But I do not wish that that money should pass into Oswald's hands. Everything my son shall have, he'll have from me.

OSWALD ALVING enters through the second door to the right; he has taken off his hat and overcoat in the hall.

My dear boy! Are you back already?

OSWALD. Yes, there's not much a man can do out of doors in this eternal rain. But I hear lunch is ready. Splendid!

REGINA enters from the dining-room with a parcel.

REGINA. [*Handing the parcel to MRS. ALVING.*] This parcel's just arrived for you, Madam.

MRS. ALVING. It'll be copies of the ode for to-morrow's ceremony.

MANDERS. Hmm…

REGINA. And lunch is served.

MRS. ALVING. Very well, we'll be straight through. I'll just—

MRS. ALVING begins to open the parcel.

REGINA. Would Mr. Alving like red or white wine?

OSWALD. Both, if you please, Miss Engstrand.

REGINA. *Bien.* Very well, sir.

REGINA exits into the dining-room.

OSWALD. I may as well help to uncork it.

OSWALD follows REGINA into the dining room, the door of which remains half open behind him.

MRS. ALVING. Yes, I thought so. Here is the Ceremonial Ode, Pastor Manders.

MANDERS. I don't know how I shall be able to deliver my speech to-morrow!

MRS. ALVING. It seems that once again you will have to display your famous strength of character.

MANDERS. Yes; it would not do to provoke scandal.

MRS. ALVING. No. But then this long, hateful farce will be over. From the day after to-morrow, I shall be able to start again as though he had never lived in this house. There shall be no one here but my boy and his mother.

From the dining-room comes the noise of a chair being overturned, and at the same moment is heard:

REGINA. [*Sharply, but in a whisper.*] Oswald! Be careful, are you mad? Let me go!

MRS. ALVING. [*Starts in terror.*] Ah—!

She stares wildly towards the half-open door. OSWALD is heard laughing and humming. A bottle is uncorked.

MANDERS. What's the matter? What is it, Mrs. Alving?

MRS. ALVING. Ghosts! The couple from the conservatory—risen again!

MANDERS. What!? —You mean Regina!? Is she—!?

MRS. ALVING. Yes. Come. Not a word—!

She seizes PASTOR MANDERS by the arm, and walks unsteadily towards the dining-room.

ACT TWO.

The same room, nothing has changed. The mist still lies heavy over the landscape.

MANDERS and MRS. ALVING enter from the dining-room.

MRS. ALVING. You're very welcome, Pastor. [*Turning back towards the dining-room.*] Aren't you joining us, Oswald?

OSWALD. [*From within.*] No, thank you. I think I'll go out for a little while.

MRS. ALVING. Yes, do. The weather seems a little brighter.

She shuts the dining-room door, goes to the hall door, and calls:

Regina!

REGINA. [*Outside.*] Yes, Mrs. Alving?

MRS. ALVING. Go down to the laundry, and give a hand with the flowers.

REGINA. Yes, Mrs. Alving.

She satisfies herself that REGINA has gone; then shuts the door.

MANDERS. He won't be able to hear us?

MRS. ALVING. Not when the door is shut. Besides, he's just going out.

MANDERS. I'm still rather shaken. I don't know how I managed to eat anything.

MRS. ALVING. No, me neither. But what are we to do?

MANDERS. Yes; what are we to do? I'm afraid I really don't know; I am so utterly inexperienced in matters of this sort.

MRS. ALVING. I'm sure that nothing serious can have happened yet.

MANDERS. Heaven forbid! But nevertheless, it is a shameful state of affairs.

MRS. ALVING. It is only an idle fancy on Oswald's part; you may be sure of that.

MANDERS. Well, as I say, I'm not accustomed to such matters. But I should certainly think that Regina—

MRS. ALVING. She must go immediately. That's as clear as daylight.

MANDERS. Yes, of course she must.

MRS. ALVING. But where to? It wouldn't be right to—

MANDERS. Where to? Home to her father, of course.

MRS. ALVING. Her father?

MANDERS. Yes, her—Oh! So then, Engstrand is not—? Good God, Mrs. Alving! But no—it's impossible! You must be mistaken after all. You see, Engstrand—

MRS. ALVING. There is no mistake, Pastor Manders. Unfortunately. Johanna confessed everything to me; and Alving could not deny it. So there was nothing to be done but have the matter hushed up.

MANDERS. No, of course. You could do nothing else.

MRS. ALVING. The girl left our service immediately, and got a good sum of money to keep quiet. The rest she managed for herself when she got to town. She renewed an old acquaintance with Engstrand, no doubt let him see that she had money in her purse, and told him some tale about a foreigner who put in here with a yacht that summer. So she and Engstrand got married straight away. Why, you married them yourself.

MANDERS. But how does that account for—? I recollect distinctly Engstrand coming to give notice of the marriage. He was quite overwhelmed with contrition, and bitterly reproached himself for what he and his fiancée had done.

MRS. ALVING. Yes; of course he had to take the blame upon himself.

MANDERS. But such a piece of duplicity on his part! And against me, too! I should never have believed it of Jacob Engstrand. I shall not fail to take him seriously to task; he may be sure of that.—And then the immorality of such a connection! And for money! How much did the girl receive?

MRS. ALVING. Sixty-five pounds.

MANDERS. Imagine that!—for a miserable sixty-five pounds, to go and marry a fallen woman!

MRS. ALVING. Then what must you think of me? I went and married a fallen man.

MANDERS. Oh, good heavens, what are you talking about!? A fallen man!

MRS. ALVING. Do you think Alving was any purer when I went with him to the altar than Johanna was when Engstrand married her?

MANDERS. But there is a world of difference between the two cases!

MRS. ALVING. Not so much difference, really—except in the price:— a miserable sixty-five pounds and a whole fortune.

MANDERS. How can you compare such totally dissimilar cases? You made your decision with regard to both your own personal feelings and those of your closest relatives.

MRS. ALVING. I thought you understood who my 'personal feelings' favoured at the time.

MANDERS. Had I understood anything of the kind, I should not have been a daily guest in your husband's house.

MRS. ALVING. At any rate, the fact remains that my feelings in no way interfered with my decision.

MANDERS. Well then, you must at least have consulted your relatives—as your duty bade you—your mother and your two aunts.

MRS. ALVING. Yes, that I certainly did. Those three set out the numbers for me. Oh, it was quite something how clearly they made out that it would be pure folly to refuse such an offer. If only mother could see me now, and know where all those riches have left me!

MANDERS. Nobody can be held responsible for the result. But this, at least, remains clear: your marriage was in full accordance with law and order.

MRS. ALVING. Oh yes, of course; law and order! I often think that's what causes all the problems in the world.

MANDERS. Mrs. Alving, that is a sinful way of talking.

MRS. ALVING. No doubt, but I won't tolerate all this constraint and insincerity any longer. I must claim my freedom.

MANDERS. What do you mean by that?

MRS. ALVING. I ought never to have concealed the facts of Alving's life. But at the time I dared not do anything else—I was afraid, partly for myself. I was such a coward.

MANDERS. A coward?

MRS. ALVING. If people had found out, they would have said—"Poor man! With a runaway wife it's no wonder he's gone astray."

MANDERS. Such remarks might have been made with a certain justification.

A beat.

MRS. ALVING. If I were braver I should go to Oswald and say, "Listen, my boy: your father was a dissolute man—"

MANDERS. Good heavens!

MRS. ALVING.—and then I should tell him all that I have told you—every word of it.

MANDERS. You quite shock me, Mrs. Alving.

MRS. ALVING. Yes; I know that. I know that all too well. I myself am shocked at the idea. I am such a coward.

MANDERS. You call it cowardice to do your duty? Have you forgotten that a son ought to love and honour his father and mother?

MRS. ALVING. Don't let us talk in such general terms. Let us ask whether Oswald ought to love and honour Chamberlain Alving.

MANDERS. Mrs. Alving, you must recognize that it would be utterly wrong for you, as a mother, to destroy your own son's ideals.

MRS. ALVING. But what about the truth?

MANDERS. But what about his ideals?

MRS. ALVING. Oh—'ideals', 'ideals'! If only I weren't such a coward!

MANDERS. Do not despise ideals, Mrs. Alving; they will avenge themselves cruelly. Take Oswald's case: he, unfortunately, seems to have few enough as it is; but I can at least see that his father stands before him as one.

MRS. ALVING. Yes, that is true.

MANDERS. And this was your own doing; you yourself created this image of his father, and nourished it, in your letters.

MRS. ALVING. Yes; in my superstitious awe of duty and propriety, I lied to my boy, year after year. Oh, what a coward—what a coward I've been!

MANDERS. You have established a happy illusion in your son's heart, Mrs. Alving; and assuredly you ought not to undervalue it.

MRS. ALVING. Hm, I wonder if you're right, Pastor—? But nevertheless, I will not have anything between him and Regina. He shall not go and wreck the poor girl's life.

MANDERS. No; good God—that would be terrible!

MRS. ALVING. If I knew he was in earnest, and that she would make him happy—

MANDERS. What? What then?

MRS. ALVING. But it could never be; sadly Regina's not that sort of woman.

MANDERS. What are you trying to say, Mrs. Alving?

MRS. ALVING. If I weren't such a pitiful coward, I should say to him, "Marry her, or make what arrangement you please, so long as there's nothing underhand about it."

MANDERS. Good heavens, would you let them marry!? Permit something so hideous—!? It would be unheard of!

MRS. ALVING. 'Unheard of'? Pastor Manders, do you really suppose that there are not several married couples in this country as closely akin as they?

MANDERS. I don't understand you at all, Mrs. Alving.

MRS. ALVING. Oh, of course you do.

MANDERS. I can only imagine that you are thinking of the possibility that—Well, yes, unfortunately family life is certainly not always as pure as it ought to be. But in such cases, one could never know—at least not with any certainty; whereas here—How can you even think of allowing your own son to—?

MRS. ALVING. But I can't! I wouldn't. Not for anything in the world; that is precisely what I'm saying.

MANDERS. No, because you are a 'coward', as you put it. But if you were not a 'coward', then what? Good God! Such a monstrous union!

MRS. ALVING. They say we are all sprung from one such union. And who was it that arranged the world so, Pastor Manders?

MANDERS. Questions of that kind I must decline to discuss with you, Mrs. Alving; you are far from being in the right frame of mind for them. But that you dare to call your scruples 'cowardly'—!

MRS. ALVING. I shall tell you what I mean by that. I am timid and faint-hearted because of the ghosts that hang about me, and that I can never quite shake off.

MANDERS. What do you say hang about you?

MRS. ALVING. Ghosts, Pastor Manders! When I heard Regina and Oswald in there, it was as though ghosts rose up before me. But I almost think we are all of us ghosts. It is not only what we have inherited from our father and mother that 'haunts' us. It is all sorts of dead ideas, and lifeless old beliefs. They have no vitality, but they cling to us all the same, and somehow we cannot shake them off. Whenever I pick up a newspaper, I seem to see them gliding between the lines. There must be ghosts all the country over, as thick as the sands of the sea. And we are all so pitifully afraid of the light.

MANDERS. So, here we have the fruits of your reading. And fine fruits they are, too! I knew these books were dangerous—freethinking, atheist propaganda!

MRS. ALVING. You are quite mistaken, my dear Pastor. In fact it was you who set me thinking; and I thank you for it with all my heart.

MANDERS. I!?

MRS. ALVING. Yes—when you forced me back under what you called 'the yoke of duty and obedience'; when you commended as right and proper that which my whole soul rejected. It was then that I began to look into the seams of your doctrines. I only wanted to pick at a single knot; but when I had got that undone, the whole thing unravelled. And then I saw how poorly sewn it really was.

MANDERS. [*Softly, with emotion.*] And was that the outcome of my life's hardest battle?

MRS. ALVING. Call it your most pitiful defeat.

MANDERS. It was my greatest victory, Helen—victory over myself.

MRS. ALVING. It was a crime against us both.

MANDERS. When you forgot yourself, and came to me crying, "Here I am; take me!" I commanded you, saying, "Woman, go home to your lawful husband." Was that a crime?

MRS. ALVING. Yes, I think it was.

MANDERS. Then we two do not understand each other.

MRS. ALVING. Not now, at any rate.

MANDERS. Never—never in my most secret thoughts have I regarded you as anything but another man's wife.

MRS. ALVING. Do you really believe that?

MANDERS. Helen—!

MRS. ALVING. People forget themselves so easily.

MANDERS. I do not. I am as I always have been.

MRS. ALVING. Well, well, well; let's not talk of old times any longer. You're now up to your ears in Boards and Committees, and I am fighting my battle with ghosts, both within and without.

MANDERS. Those without I shall help you lay to rest. After all the terrible things I have heard from you to-day, I cannot in conscience permit an unprotected girl to remain in your house.

MRS. ALVING. Don't you think the best plan would be to get her settled?—suitably married, I mean.

MANDERS. Undoubtedly. I think it would be desirable for her in every respect. Regina is now at the age when—Of course I don't know much about these things, but—

MRS. ALVING. Regina matured very early.

MANDERS. Yes, I thought so. I seem to remember that she was remarkably well developed when I prepared her for confirmation. But in the meantime, she ought to be at home with her father—Ah! But of course, Engstrand isn't—! Oh, how could he!?—How could he lie to me like that?

There is a knock at the door that leads from the hall.

MRS. ALVING. Who can this be? Come in!

ENGSTRAND enters wearing his Sunday clothes, and remains in the doorway.

ENGSTRAND. I humbly beg your pardon, but—

MANDERS. Hm!

MRS. ALVING. Is that you, Engstrand?

ENGSTRAND.—none of the servants were about, so I took the liberty of knocking.

MRS. ALVING. Oh, very well. Come in. Do you want to speak to me?

ENGSTRAND. [*Coming in.*] Uh, no, I'm obliged to you, ma'am; it was with his Reverence I wanted to have a word or two.

MANDERS. Oh! You want to speak to me, do you?

ENGSTRAND. Yes, I'd very much like to—

MANDERS. Well; may I ask what you want?

ENGSTRAND. Well, it was just this, your Reverence: we've been paid off down at the Orphanage—my grateful thanks to you, ma'am,—and now everything's finished, I've been thinking it would only be right and proper for us, since we've been working so honestly together all this time—well, I was thinking we ought to finish up with a little prayer-meeting to-night.

MANDERS. A prayer-meeting? Down at the Orphanage?

ENGSTRAND. Oh, if your Reverence doesn't think it proper—

MANDERS. Oh yes, I do; but, er...

ENGSTRAND. I've been in the habit of offering up a little prayer in the evenings, myself—

MRS. ALVING. Have you?

ENGSTRAND. Yes, every now and then just a little edification, in a manner of speaking. But I'm a poor, common man, and don't really have the gift for it, God help me!—and so I thought, as the Reverend Pastor Manders happened to be here, I'd—

MANDERS. Just a moment, Engstrand. Firstly I must ask you whether you are in the right frame of mind for such a meeting. Do you feel your conscience clear and at ease?

ENGSTRAND. Oh, God help us, your Reverence! We'd better not talk about conscience.

MANDERS. Yes, that is precisely what we must talk about. What have you to answer?

ENGSTRAND. Why... a man's conscience... ah, it can be bad enough now and then.

MANDERS. Oh, so you admit that. Then perhaps you will make a clean breast of it, and tell me—what is the truth about Regina?

MRS. ALVING. [*Quickly.*] Pastor Manders!

MANDERS. [*Reassuringly.*] Please allow me—

ENGSTRAND. About Regina! Lord, you frightened the life out of me! [*Looks at MRS. ALVING.*] There's nothing wrong with Regina, is there?

MANDERS. We shall hope not. But I am asking you for the truth about you and her. You're her father are you?

ENGSTRAND. [*Uncertain.*] Well, er... your Reverence knows all about me and poor Johanna.

MANDERS. Come now, no more prevarication! Your wife told Mrs. Alving the whole story before quitting her service.

ENGSTRAND. Did she, now? Well, I'll be—

MANDERS. You see, we know you now, Engstrand.

ENGSTRAND. And she swore! Took her Bible oath!

MANDERS. She swore on the Bible!?

ENGSTRAND. Well, no, perhaps not; but she did swear! And solemnly, too.

MANDERS. And you have hidden the truth from me for all these years? From me! Who has trusted you without reserve!

ENGSTRAND. I'm afraid so.

MANDERS. Have I deserved this of you, Engstrand? Have I not always been ready to help you in word and deed, so far as it lay in my power? Answer me. Have I not?

ENGSTRAND. Aye, that's true enough. Many a time I should have made a bad end were it not for you, your Reverence.

MANDERS. And this is how you reward me! You cause me to enter falsehoods in the Church Register, and you withhold from me, year after year, the explanations you owed alike to me and to the truth. Your conduct has been wholly inexcusable, Engstrand; and from this moment on I shall have nothing more to do with you!

ENGSTRAND. [*With a sigh.*] Yes, I suppose there's no helping it.

MANDERS. Well, you can't possibly justify your actions.

ENGSTRAND. Who'd 'a thought she'd go and make a bad thing worse by talking about it? Now, your Reverence, if you were just t'imagine yourself in the same trouble as poor Johanna—

MANDERS. I!?

ENGSTRAND. Oh, Lord bless you, I don't mean exactly the same! But, if your Reverence had anything to be ashamed of in the eyes of the world, as the saying goes. We men oughtn't judge a poor woman too harshly, your Reverence.

MANDERS. I am doing nothing of the sort. It is you I am reproaching.

ENGSTRAND. Might I make so bold as to ask your Reverence a question?

MANDERS. If you must.

ENGSTRAND. Isn't it right and proper for a man to raise up the fallen?

MANDERS. It certainly is.

ENGSTRAND. And isn't a man bound to keep his word?

MANDERS. Why yes, of course he is; but—

ENGSTRAND. So when Johanna had got into trouble by that Norwegian—or it might have been a Dane or a Swede, as they call them—but either way, you see, she came back to town. Poor thing, she'd sent me about my business once or twice before: for she couldn't bear the sight of anything as wasn't handsome; and I'd got this poor leg of mine. Your Reverence'll remember how I ventured up into a dance hall, where sailors were carrying on with drink and devilry, as the saying goes. And how, when I tried to show them the error of their ways—

MRS. ALVING. Ha!

MANDERS. I know all about it, Engstrand; the ruffians threw you downstairs. You have told me of the affair already; your infirmity is of great credit to you.

ENGSTRAND. I didn't mean to boast about it, your Reverence, I only meant to say that when she came and confessed everything to me, with weeping and gnashing of teeth, I can tell your Reverence; it broke my heart to hear it.

MANDERS. Did it indeed? Well, go on.

ENGSTRAND. So I says to her, "That Dane, he's still sailing about on the boundless ocean. But you, Johanna," says I, "you've committed a grievous sin, and you're a fallen creature. But Jacob Engstrand," says I, "he knows how to stand on his own two feet!" —Well, figuratively speaking, your Reverence.

MANDERS. Yes, I understand you quite well. Go on.

ENGSTRAND. Well, that was how I raised her up and made an honest woman of her. So as folks shouldn't get to know how she'd gone astray with foreigners.

MANDERS. In that you acted very honourably. But I cannot approve of your stooping to take money—

ENGSTRAND. Money? I? Not a farthing!

MANDERS. [*Inquiringly to MRS. ALVING.*] But—

ENGSTRAND. Oh, wait a minute!—now I remember. Johanna did have a few shillings. But I wouldn't have anything to do with it. "Oh, no!" says I, "that's mammon; that's the wages of sin! This wretched gold"—or notes, or whatever it was—"we'll just fling that right back in that Dane's face," says I. But already he was off and away, over the stormy sea, your Reverence.

MANDERS. Is that so, my dear Engstrand?

ENGSTRAND. It is indeed, sir. So Johanna and I, we agreed that the money should go to the child's education; and so it did, and I can account for every blessèd farthing of it.

MANDERS. Why, this alters matters considerably.

ENGSTRAND. That's just how it was, your Reverence. And I make so bold as to say I've been a good father to Regina, in my own way; for I'm no more than a weak vessel, I'm afraid!

MANDERS. Well, well, my good man—

ENGSTRAND. Nevertheless, I have brought up the child, and lived kindly with poor Johanna, and ruled over my own house, as the Scripture has it. But it would never occur to me to go to your Reverence and bluster and boast because even the likes of me had done some good in the world. Oh, no, sir; when anything of that sort happens to Jacob Engstrand, he holds his tongue about it! Though I daresay it doesn't happen all that often. And when I do come to see your Reverence, I find a mortal deal that's wicked and weak to talk about. For I've said it before, and I'll say it again—a man's conscience isn't always as clear as it might be.

MANDERS. Jacob Engstrand, give me your hand.

ENGSTRAND. Oh, Lord! Your Reverence—

MANDERS. Come, none of that [*wrings his hand*]. There we are!

ENGSTRAND. And if I might humbly beg your Reverence's pardon—

MANDERS. You? Why, on the contrary, it is I who must beg your pardon—

ENGSTRAND. Oh, no, Sir; good heavens!

MANDERS. Yes, most certainly. And I do it with all my heart. Forgive me for misunderstanding you. If you would accept my sincerest regrets and my goodwill towards you, I should be much indebted to you.

ENGSTRAND. Indebted?

MANDERS. Indeed, my dear Engstrand.

ENGSTRAND. Well, there is something you might do for me, your Reverence. You see, with the bit of money I've saved up here, I was thinking I might set up a Sailors' Home back in town.

MRS. ALVING. You?

ENGSTRAND. Yes; it might be a sort of Orphanage, too, in a manner of speaking. There are so many temptations for seafaring folk ashore. But in this Home of mine, a man might feel as if he was under a father's eye, I was thinking.

MANDERS. Well, what do you say to this, Mrs. Alving?

ENGSTRAND. Lord knows, it's not a huge amount I've got to start with, but if I could only find a helping hand, why—

MANDERS. Yes, yes; we will look into the matter more closely. It strikes me as a very admirable project. But now, you go on ahead; tidy up, get the candles lighted, get the place fit for worship. We shall pass an edifying hour together, my good man; for now I can quite believe you are in the right frame of mind.

ENGSTRAND. I daresay I am, your Reverence. And so I'll say good-bye, ma'am, and thank you kindly; and take good care of Regina for me— [*Wipes a tear from his eye*]—poor Johanna's child. It's a queer thing, but I've come to love her as if she were my own flesh and blood, you know? I truly have.

He bows and goes out through the hall.

MANDERS. Well, what do you say of him now, Mrs. Alving? That was a very different account of matters, was it not?

MRS. ALVING. Yes, it certainly was.

MANDERS. It goes to show how extremely wary one must be of judging one's fellow creatures. But what a profound joy it is to discover that one has been mistaken! Don't you agree, Mrs. Alving?

MRS. ALVING. I think you are, and always will be, a great baby, Manders.

MANDERS. I?

MRS. ALVING. [*Laying her hands upon his shoulders.*] And I tell you I have half a mind to put my arms around your neck, and kiss you.

MANDERS. [*Retreating.*] Good God, no! What an idea!

MRS. ALVING. [*With a smile.*] Oh, you needn't be afraid of me.

MANDERS. [*Behind the table.*] You have sometimes such an exaggerated way of expressing yourself. Now, let me just collect all the documents, and put them in my bag. [*He does so.*] There, that's all in order. And now, good-bye for the present. Keep your eyes open when Oswald comes back. I shall look in again later.

He takes his hat and goes out through the hall door. MRS. ALVING sighs, looks for a moment out of the window, sets the room in order a little, and is about to go into the dining-room, but stops at the door with a half-suppressed cry.

MRS. ALVING. Oswald, are you still there?

OSWALD. [*In the dining room.*] I'm only finishing my cigar.

MRS. ALVING. I thought you had gone for a walk.

OSWALD. In this weather?

A glass clinks. MRS. ALVING leaves the door open, and sits down with her knitting on the sofa by the window.

Was that Pastor Manders that went out just now?

MRS. ALVING. Yes; he went down to the Orphanage.

OSWALD. Hmm.

The glass and decanter clink again.

MRS. ALVING. Oswald, my dear, you should be careful with that whisky. It is strong.

OSWALD. Keeps out the damp.

MRS. ALVING. Wouldn't you rather come and sit with me?

OSWALD. I thought I couldn't smoke in there.

MRS. ALVING. You know quite well you may smoke cigars.

OSWALD. Oh, all right then; I'll come through. Just one last drop… There!

He comes into the room with his cigar, and shuts the door after him. A short silence.

Where did the pastor go?

MRS. ALVING. I've just told you; he went down to the Orphanage.

OSWALD. Oh, yes; so you did.

MRS. ALVING. You shouldn't stay so long at the table, Oswald.

OSWALD. But I find it so pleasant, mother. Just think what it is for me to come home and sit at mother's table, in mother's room, and eat mother's delicious dishes.

MRS. ALVING. Oh, my dear boy!

OSWALD. Besides, what else can I do with myself here? I can't do any work.

MRS. ALVING. Why not?

OSWALD. In this perpetual grey? All day without a single ray of sunshine! And not being able to work, it's—Urrgh!

MRS. ALVING. Perhaps you shouldn't have come home?

OSWALD. Oh, yes, mother; I had to.

MRS. ALVING. You know I would ten times rather forgo the joy of having you here, than let you—

OSWALD. Tell me, mother: does it really make you so very happy to have me home again?

36

MRS. ALVING. Does it make me happy!?

OSWALD. I should have thought it would be pretty much the same to you whether I was here or not.

MRS. ALVING. How can you have the heart to say that to your own mother, Oswald?

OSWALD. But you've got on very well without me all this time.

MRS. ALVING. Yes; I have got on without you. That is true.

A silence. Twilight slowly begins to fall. OSWALD paces to and fro across the room. He has laid his cigar down.

OSWALD. May I sit beside you, Mother?

MRS. ALVING. Yes, do, my dear boy.

OSWALD. [*Sits down.*] Mother, there is something I must tell you.

MRS. ALVING. [*Anxiously.*] Well?

OSWALD. For I can't go on hiding it any longer.

MRS. ALVING. Hiding what? What is it, my son?

OSWALD. I could never bring myself to write to you about it; and since I've come home—

MRS. ALVING. [*Seizes him by the arm.*] Oswald, what's the matter?

OSWALD. Both yesterday and to-day I have tried to put the thoughts out of my mind—to cast them off; but it's no use.

MRS. ALVING. [*Rising.*] You must tell me what you mean, Oswald!

OSWALD. [*Draws her down to the sofa again.*] Sit still; and I shall try to tell you.—I complained of fatigue after my journey—

MRS. ALVING. Yes, I remember.

OSWALD. But it isn't that that's the matter with me; at least, it's no ordinary fatigue—

MRS. ALVING. [*Tries to jump up.*] You're not ill, are you, Oswald?

OSWALD. [*Draws her down again.*] Sit still, mother. Try not to get hysterical. Now I'm not downright ill, either; not what is commonly called 'ill'. Mother, my mind is broken—ruined—I shall never be able to work again!

With his hands before his face, he buries his head in her lap, and breaks into bitter sobbing.

MRS. ALVING. Oswald! Look at me! No! No, it's not true.

OSWALD. I'll never work again! Never!—never! A living death! Mother, can you imagine anything so dreadful?

MRS. ALVING. My poor boy! How has this happened?

OSWALD. [*Sitting upright again.*] Well that's just it; I don't know! I can't possibly understand it. I've never led what might be called a dissolute life. You mustn't think that of me, mother! I've never done that.

MRS. ALVING. I'm sure you haven't, Oswald.

OSWALD. And yet this has happened all the same—this terrible mistake!

MRS. ALVING. But it will pass, my beautiful blessèd boy. It's nothing but over-work, that is all. Believe me.

OSWALD. I thought so too, at first; but no.

MRS. ALVING. Then you must tell me everything.

OSWALD. Yes, I will.

MRS. ALVING. When did you first notice it?

OSWALD. It was just after the last time I'd been home, once I'd got back to Paris again. I began to feel the most violent pains in my head—chiefly in the back of my head, or so it seemed. It was as though an iron ring was being screwed around my neck and the base of my skull.

MRS. ALVING. What then?

OSWALD. At first I thought it was just a return of those headaches I had been plagued with while I was growing up—

MRS. ALVING. Yes! Yes, that would—

OSWALD. But it wasn't that. I soon found that out. I couldn't work anymore. I wanted to start on a big new picture, but my powers seemed to fail me. All my strength was crippled, and I could form no definite images; everything just seemed to swim before my eyes. Oh, it was awful! Eventually I sent for a doctor—and from him I learnt the truth.

MRS. ALVING. How do you mean?

OSWALD. He was one of the finest doctors in Paris. I told him my symptoms; and then he set to work asking me a string of questions which I thought had nothing to do with the matter. I couldn't imagine what the man was after—

MRS. ALVING. Well?

OSWALD. At last he said: "There has been something rotten in you from the day of your birth." The actual word he used was *vermoulu* – worm eaten.

MRS. ALVING. What did he mean by that?

OSWALD. I didn't understand him either, and begged him to explain himself more clearly. And then the old cynic said—Oh—!

MRS. ALVING. What did he say?

OSWALD. He said, "The sins of the fathers are visited upon the children."

MRS. ALVING. [*Rising slowly.*] The sins of the fathers—!?

OSWALD. I very nearly struck him in the face—

MRS. ALVING. [*Walks away across the room.*] The sins of the fathers—

OSWALD. [*Smiles sadly.*] Yes; what do you think of that? Of course I assured him that such a thing was out of the question. But do you think he gave in? No, he stuck to it; and it was only when I produced your letters and translated the passages relating to father—

MRS. ALVING. But then—?

OSWALD. Then of course he had to admit that he was on the wrong track; and so I learnt the truth—the incomprehensible truth! I ought never to have joined my comrades in that free and glorious life of theirs. It had been too much for my strength. I had brought it all upon myself!

MRS. ALVING. Oswald! No, no; do not believe it!

OSWALD. He said there could be no other explanation. That's the worst part of it. Incurably ruined for life—and by my own recklessness! All that I hoped to do in the world—I can't bear to think of it anymore—I'm not even able to think of it. Oh! if only I could undo everything and start all over again!

He buries his face in the sofa. There is a silence. After a while, OSWALD looks up and continues:

If only it had been something inherited—something I, at least, wasn't responsible for! But this! To have so shamefully—so thoughtlessly!— thrown away my own happiness, health, everything!—my future, my life!

MRS. ALVING. Hush, hush! My dear, darling boy! It's not possible. Things are not so desperate as you think.

OSWALD. Oh, you don't know—[*Springs up.*] And then, mother, to cause you all this grief! Many a time I've almost wished that, deep down, you didn't really care about me at all.

MRS. ALVING. Oswald! You're my only son! You're all I have in the world; the only thing I care about!

OSWALD. Yes, yes, I see that now. When I'm at home, I see it, of course I do; and that's almost the hardest part.—But now you've heard the whole story so we won't talk any more about it to-day. I daren't spend too long thinking about it. Get me something to drink, mother.

MRS. ALVING. To drink? What do you want to drink now?

OSWALD. Oh, anything you like. You have some ale in the house.

MRS. ALVING. Yes, but my dear Oswald—

OSWALD. Oh, don't refuse me, mother, please. Be kind! I must have something to wash away all these restless thoughts.

He goes into the conservatory.

And then it's so dark all the time!

MRS. ALVING pulls a bell-rope on the right.

And this endless rain! It may go on for weeks and weeks—months even! We'll never get a glimpse of sunlight! In all the times I've been at home, I don't once remember seeing the sun shine.

MRS. ALVING. Oh, Oswald, you're thinking of leaving me, aren't you?

OSWALD. Hm?—Oh, I'm not thinking of anything. I can't think of anything! I've had to leave thinking alone.

REGINA enters from the dining-room.

REGINA. Did you ring, madam?

MRS. ALVING. Yes; bring in the lamp, Regina.

REGINA. Right away, madam. It's already lit.

REGINA exits to fetch the lamp.

MRS. ALVING. Oswald, be frank with me.

OSWALD. And so I have been, mother. I think I have told you enough.

REGINA re-enters with the lamp and sets it on the table.

MRS. ALVING. Regina, you may bring us a small bottle of champagne.

REGINA. Very well, madam.

REGINA goes out to get the champagne.

OSWALD. [*Putting his arms around MRS. ALVING's neck.*] Just what I wanted. I knew mother wouldn't let her boy go thirsty.

MRS. ALVING. My poor, darling Oswald; how could I deny you anything now?

OSWALD. Is that true, mother? Do you mean it?

MRS. ALVING. Mean what?

OSWALD. That you couldn't deny me anything.

MRS. ALVING. Oswald, my dear—

OSWALD. Hush!

REGINA enters carrying a tray with a half-bottle of champagne and two glasses on it. She sets the tray on the table.

REGINA. Shall I open it?

OSWALD. No, thanks. I'll do it myself.

REGINA goes out again. MRS. ALVING sits at the table.

MRS. ALVING. What was it you meant: I mustn't deny you?

OSWALD. [*Opening the bottle.*] First let's have a glass—or two.

The cork pops. He pours champagne into the two glasses, and offers one to MRS. ALVING.

MRS. ALVING. Not for me, thank you.

OSWALD. Oh! won't you? Then I will!

He drinks both glasses and then joins MRS. ALVING at the table.

MRS. ALVING. Well?

OSWALD. Tell me—I thought you and Pastor Manders seemed very quiet at lunch to-day. It was rather strange.

MRS. ALVING. You noticed?

OSWALD. Yes.

A short silence.

Tell me: what do you think of Regina?

MRS. ALVING. What do I think?

OSWALD. Yes; isn't she wonderful?

MRS. ALVING. My dear Oswald, you don't know her as well as I do—

OSWALD. Well?

A beat.

MRS. ALVING. Unfortunately Regina was allowed to stay at home for too long. I ought to have taken her earlier into my house.

OSWALD. Yes, but isn't she wonderful to look at, mother?

He refills his glass.

MRS. ALVING. Regina has many serious faults—

OSWALD. Oh, what does that matter?

He drinks again.

MRS. ALVING. But I am fond of her, nevertheless, and I am responsible for her. I will do everything I can to keep her out of harm's way.

OSWALD. [*Springs up.*] Mother, Regina is my only salvation!

MRS. ALVING. [*Rising.*] What do you mean by that?

OSWALD. I can't bear all this suffering alone.

MRS. ALVING. Have you not your mother to bear it with you?

OSWALD. Yes; that's what I thought; and so I came home to you. But that just won't do—I can see that it won't. I cannot stand my life here.

MRS. ALVING. Oswald!

41

OSWALD. I must live differently, mother. That's why I must leave you; I won't have you looking on at it.

MRS. ALVING. My poor boy! But, Oswald, while you are so ill as this—

OSWALD. If it were only the illness, I should stay with you, mother; for you are the best friend I have in all the world.

MRS. ALVING. And so I am, Oswald! I am, aren't I?

OSWALD. But it's all the torment, the terrible remorse—and then, that great, mortal dread. Oh—it's awful!

MRS. ALVING. Dread? What dread? What do you mean?

OSWALD. Oh, you mustn't ask me any more. I don't know, I can't describe it.

MRS. ALVING goes over to the right and pulls the bell.

What is it you want?

MRS. ALVING. I want my boy to be happy—that is what I want. He shan't go on torturing himself like this.

REGINA appears at the door. MRS. ALVING addresses her:

More champagne—a large bottle.

REGINA goes.

OSWALD. Mother!

MRS. ALVING. Do you think we don't know how to live out here?

OSWALD. Oh, isn't she wonderful to look at!

MRS. ALVING. [*Siting by the table.*] Sit down, Oswald; we must talk seriously for a moment.

OSWALD sits.

OSWALD. Well, I daresay you don't know, mother, but I owe Regina some reparation.

MRS. ALVING. You—?

OSWALD. For a bit of thoughtlessness, or whatever you like to call it— very innocent, at any rate. When I was home last...

MRS. ALVING. What!?

OSWALD. She often used to ask me about Paris, and I used to tell her a thing or two. Then one day I happened to say to her, "Shouldn't you like to go there yourself?"

MRS. ALVING. Well?

OSWALD. She blushed, and then she said, "Yes, I should like it very much." "Well," I replied, "it might perhaps be managed"—or something to that effect.

MRS. ALVING. And then?

OSWALD. Of course I had forgotten all about it; but the day before yesterday I happened to ask her whether she was glad I was to stay at home for so long—

MRS. ALVING. Yes?

OSWALD. And then she gave me such a strange look, and asked, "But what's to become of my trip to Paris?"

MRS. ALVING. Her trip!

OSWALD. And so it transpired that she had taken the matter seriously; that she had been thinking of me the whole time, and had even begun to learn French—

MRS. ALVING. So that was why—!

OSWALD. But mother, when she stood there before me—so fresh and lovely—till then I had hardly noticed her, but in that moment... it was as if she was standing there with open arms—

MRS. ALVING. Oswald!

OSWALD.—then it finally dawned on me that my salvation lay in her; for she was full of the joy of life.

MRS. ALVING. [*Starts.*] The joy of life? Can there be salvation in that?

REGINA enters from the dining room, with a bottle of champagne.

REGINA. I'm sorry to have been so long; I had to go down to the cellar.

She places the bottle on the table.

OSWALD. Bring another glass.

REGINA. [*Surprised.*] Mrs. Alving already has a glass, sir.

OSWALD. Yes, but bring one for yourself, Regina.

REGINA starts and gives a rapid side glance at MRS. ALVING.

What's the matter?

REGINA. [*Softly and hesitatingly.*] Does Mrs. Alving—?

MRS. ALVING. Bring the glass, Regina.

REGINA goes out into the dining-room.

OSWALD. [*Following her with his eyes.*] Have you noticed the way she walks?—so firmly and lightly!

MRS. ALVING. This cannot be, Oswald!

OSWALD. It's already settled. Can't you see that? It's no use setting yourself up against it.

REGINA enters with an empty glass, which she keeps in her hand.

Sit down, Regina.

REGINA looks inquiringly at MRS. ALVING.

MRS. ALVING. Sit down.

REGINA sits on a chair by the dining room door, still holding the empty glass in her hand.

Oswald—what was it you were saying about the joy of life?

OSWALD. Ah, the joy of life, mother—that's something you don't know much about in these parts. I've never felt it here.

MRS. ALVING. Not when you're with me?

OSWALD. Not when I'm at home. But you wouldn't understand.

MRS. ALVING. Oh, yes; I think I almost do understand it now.

OSWALD. And also, the joy of work! It's the same thing, really. But that too, you know nothing about.

MRS. ALVING. Perhaps you're right. Tell me about it, then, Oswald.

OSWALD. I only mean that here people are brought up to believe that work is a curse and a punishment for sin, and that life is something miserable; something it would be best to have done with, and the sooner the better.

MRS. ALVING. 'A vale of tears', yes; and we certainly do our best to make it one.

OSWALD. But out in the great, free world people won't hear of such things! There nobody really believes such doctrines any longer. Out there you feel it's a positive bliss—an ecstasy!—merely to draw the breath of life. Mother, have you never noticed that everything I have painted has turned upon the joy of life?—always, always upon the joy of life?—light and sunshine and glorious air!—and faces radiant with happiness! That's why I'm afraid of remaining at home with you.

MRS. ALVING. Afraid? What are you afraid of here, with me?

OSWALD. I'm afraid lest all my instincts should be warped into ugliness.

MRS. ALVING. You think that's what would happen?

OSWALD. I know it. Even if I were to try and live the same life here as there, it would never truly be the same.

MRS. ALVING. [*Standing.*] Now I see.

OSWALD. What is it you see?

MRS. ALVING. I see it now for the first time. And now I can speak.

OSWALD. [*Standing.*] Mother, I don't understand you.

REGINA. [*Also standing.*] Perhaps I ought to go?

MRS. ALVING. No. Stay here. Now I can speak. Now, my boy, you shall know the whole truth. And then you can choose. Oswald, Regina...

OSWALD. Wait! Here comes the Pastor—

MANDERS enters by the hall door.

MANDERS. Well! We have had a most edifying time down there.

OSWALD. As have we.

MANDERS. We must assist Engstrand with his Sailors' Home. And Regina must go and help him—

REGINA. No thank you, sir.

MANDERS. [*Noticing her for the first tine.*] What on earth are you doing here? And with a glass in your hand!

REGINA. [*Hastily putting the glass down.*] Pardon me!

OSWALD. Regina is leaving with me, Pastor Manders.

MANDERS. Leaving! With you!?

OSWALD. Yes; as my wife—if she wishes it.

MANDERS. But, good Lord—!

REGINA. It's not my doing, sir.

OSWALD. Or she'll stay here, if I stay.

REGINA. Here!?

MANDERS. I am thunderstruck at your conduct, Mrs. Alving.

MRS. ALVING. They will do nothing of the sort; for now I shall speak out plainly.

MANDERS. No, no, no! Mrs. Alving, you mustn't!

MRS. ALVING. Yes, Pastor Manders, I must and I will. And no ideals shall suffer after all.

OSWALD. What is it, mother? What are you hiding?

REGINA. Mrs. Alving, listen! There are shouts coming from outside!

She goes into the conservatory and looks out. OSWALD goes to the window on the left.

OSWALD. What's going on? Where's all that light coming from?

REGINA. [*Cries out.*] The Orphanage is on fire!

MRS. ALVING. [*Rushing to the window.*] On fire!?

MANDERS. On fire? Impossible! I've just come from there.

OSWALD. Where's my hat? Oh, damn it!—Father's Orphanage—!

He rushes out through the garden door.

MRS. ALVING. My shawl, Regina! Quickly; the whole place is ablaze!

MANDERS. Terrible! Mrs. Alving, this is a judgment on this wicked house.

MRS. ALVING. I'm sure you're right, Pastor. Come, Regina.

She and REGINA exit hurriedly through the hall. MANDERS is left alone.

MANDERS. And not insured!

He goes out the same way.

ACT THREE.

The room as before. All the doors stand open. The lamp is still burning on the table. It is dark outside; there is only a faint glow from the remains of the fire which can be seen in the background to the left.

MRS. ALVING, with a shawl over her head, stands in the conservatory, looking out. REGINA, also with a shawl on, stands a little behind her.

MRS. ALVING. The whole thing burnt—burnt to the ground!

REGINA. It's still burning in the basement.

MRS. ALVING. Why doesn't Oswald come home? There's nothing to be saved.

REGINA. Would you like me to take him his hat?

MRS. ALVING. Didn't he take it?

REGINA. No; it's in the hall.

MRS. ALVING. Leave it; he must be on his way now. —I'll go and look for him.

She goes out through the garden door and a few moments later MANDERS comes in from the hall.

MANDERS. Is Mrs. Alving not here?

REGINA. She's just gone out through the garden.

MANDERS. This is the most terrible night I've ever experienced.

REGINA. It's a dreadful misfortune, isn't it, sir?

MANDERS. Oh, let's not mention it! I can't bear to think of it any longer.

REGINA. But how could such a thing have happened?

MANDERS. Don't ask me, Miss Engstrand! How should I know? Are you also—? Is it not enough that your father—?

REGINA. What about him?

MANDERS. Oh, he has been quite insufferable to-night—

ENGSTRAND enters through the hall.

ENGSTRAND. Your Reverence—

MANDERS. Oh! Must you hound me like this, man?

ENGSTRAND. Yes, God help me, but I must! Good Lord, this is a terrible ugly business, your Reverence.

MANDERS. Dreadful, dreadful!

REGINA. What's all this?

ENGSTRAND. Well, it all came out of this evening's prayer-meeting, you see. [*Softly.*] We've got him now, my girl. [*Aloud.*] And to think that it should be at my instigation that the good Pastor should be to blame for all this!

MANDERS. But, Engstrand, I can assure you—

ENGSTRAND. There wasn't another soul save your Reverence that laid so much as a finger on the candles.

MANDERS. So you claim. But I certainly cannot recall ever having a candle in my hand.

ENGSTRAND. But I saw as clear as daylight how your Reverence took the candle, snuffed it with your fingers, then threw the wick away into the shavings.

MANDERS. And you saw me do it?

ENGSTRAND. That's right; I saw it as plain as the nose on your face.

MANDERS. I can't understand it; it's never been my habit to snuff candles with my fingers.

ENGSTRAND. Aye, and awful risky it looked, too! But is it really as bad as they're saying, your Reverence?

MANDERS. [*Restlessly walking back and forth.*] Oh, don't ask me!

ENGSTRAND. [*Walking with him.*] And your Reverence hadn't insured it, either?

MANDERS. [*Continuing to walk up and down.*] No, I hadn't, I hadn't; I've told you already.

ENGSTRAND. [*Following him.*] Not insured! And then to go straight down and set light to the whole thing! Lord, Lord, what a disaster!

MANDERS. [Wipes the sweat from his forehead.] Aye, you may well say that, Engstrand.

ENGSTRAND. And to think that such a thing should happen to a benevolent Institution! One that was to have been a blessing both to town and country, as the saying goes! Oh, the newspapers won't be for handling your Reverence very gently, I expect.

MANDERS. No; that's just what I'm thinking. That's almost the worst part of it. All the hateful attacks and incriminations—! Oh, it makes me shudder to think of it!

MRS. ALVING comes in from the garden.

MRS. ALVING. He's determined to stay down there.

MANDERS. Ah, there you are, Mrs. Alving.

MRS. ALVING. So, you have escaped your speech, Pastor Manders.

48

MANDERS. Oh, well, I would be glad to—

MRS. ALVING. [*Quietly.*] It's for the best. That Orphanage wouldn't have done anyone any good.

MANDERS. You think not?

MRS. ALVING. Do you think it would?

MANDERS. All the same, it's a terrible misfortune.

MRS. ALVING. Let us speak of it plainly, as a matter of business.— Are you waiting for the Pastor, Engstrand?

ENGSTRAND. That's right, ma'am.

MRS. ALVING. Then take a seat and wait for a moment.

ENGSTRAND. Thank you, ma'am; I'd rather stand.

MRS. ALVING. [*To MANDERS.*] I suppose you're going by the steamer?

MANDERS. Yes; it leaves in an hour.

MRS. ALVING. Then be so good as to take all the papers with you. I don't wish to hear another word of this affair. I have other things to think of.

MANDERS. Mrs. Alving—

MRS. ALVING. Later on I shall send you a Power of Attorney to settle everything as you please.

MANDERS. That I will very readily undertake. I'm afraid the original destination of the endowment must now be completely changed.

MRS. ALVING. Of course it must.

MANDERS. Yes… first of all, I think I shall arrange for the Sunhill property to pass to the parish. The land is by no means without value; they might be able to put it to good use. And the interest on the money in the bank I could, perhaps, redirect towards some other benevolent Institution, either here or in town

MRS. ALVING. You may do as you please. I no longer have any interest in the matter.

ENGSTRAND. Spare a thought for my Sailors' Home, your Reverence.

MANDERS. Upon my word, that is not a bad suggestion. That must be considered.

ENGSTRAND. Oh, to hell with considering—Good God!

MANDERS. Well, sadly I cannot tell how long I shall be able to retain control of these affairs—whether public opinion may not compel me to step down. It entirely depends on the result of the official inquiry—

MRS. ALVING. What are you talking about?

MANDERS. —and that can by no means be foretold.

ENGSTRAND. [*Drawing nearer to him.*] Aye, but it can though. For here stands old Jacob Engstrand.

MANDERS. Well, yes, but—?

ENGSTRAND. [*More softy.*] And Jacob Engstrand isn't the sort to abandon a friend in his hour of need, as the saying goes.

MANDERS. Yes, but my good fellow, how—?

ENGSTRAND. Jacob Engstrand may even be likened to a sort of guardian angel, your Reverence.

MANDERS. Oh no, I'm sorry, Engstrand, but that really is unacceptable.

ENGSTRAND. Oh, that'll be the way of it, all the same. For I know a man who's taken on the sins of others once before.

A beat.

MANDERS. Jacob! [*Wrings his hand.*] Oh! Yours is a rare nature. Well, you shall be helped with your Sailors' Home; you can count on me for that.

ENGSTRAND tries to thank him, but cannot for emotion. MANDERS then hangs his travelling-bag over his shoulder and prepares to leave.

And now let us set out. We two shall go together.

ENGSTRAND. [*Softly to REGINA.*] You come along too, my lass, and you'll be as snug as the yolk in an egg.

REGINA. *Merci!*

She goes out into the hall and fetches MANDERS' overcoat.

MANDERS. Good-bye, Mrs. Alving! And may the spirit of Law and Order soon light upon this house.

MRS. ALVING. Good-bye, Pastor Manders.

She sees OSWALD coming in through the garden door and goes towards the conservatory to meet him. ENGSTRAND and REGINA help MANDERS to get his coat on, and ENGSTRAND takes the opportunity to address her:

ENGSTRAND. Farewell, my child. And if ever you're in any trouble, you know where Jacob Engstrand is to be found. [*Softly.*] Little Harbour Street, eh? [*To MRS. ALVING and OSWALD.*] And the refuge for wandering mariners shall be called 'Chamberlain Alving's Home!' Aye, that it shall. And if it please the Lord for me to run that house in my own way, I make so bold as to promise that it shall be worthy of the good Chamberlain's memory.

An uncomfortable beat.

MANDERS. Yes, er… Come along, my dear Engstrand. Good-bye! Good-bye!

He and ENGSTRAND go out through the hall.

OSWALD. What's this 'Home' he was talking about?

MRS. ALVING. Oh, it's a kind of shelter that he and Pastor Manders want to set up.

OSWALD. It will burn down like the other.

MRS. ALVING. What makes you say that?

OSWALD. Everything will burn. All trace of father will be wiped out. Here I am, burning down as well.

REGINA starts and looks at him.

MRS. ALVING. Oswald, my poor boy! You shouldn't have stayed down there for so long.

OSWALD. [*Sitting down by the table.*] I think you might be right about that.

MRS. ALVING. Let me dry your face, Oswald; you're all wet.

She dries his face with her pocket-handkerchief.

OSWALD. Thank you, mother.

MRS. ALVING. Are you not tired, Oswald? Wouldn't you like to sleep?

OSWALD. No, no—I don't sleep! I never sleep, I only pretend to. It'll come soon enough.

MRS. ALVING. Oh, my darling boy, you really are ill, aren't you?

REGINA. Mr. Alving's ill?

OSWALD. [*Impatiently.*] Oh, do shut the doors! This mortal dread—

MRS. ALVING. Shut the doors, Regina.

REGINA shuts them and remains standing by the hall door. MRS. ALVING takes her shawl off: REGINA does the same. MRS. ALVING draws a chair across to OSWALD'S, and sits by him.

MRS. ALVING. There now! I'm going to sit beside you.

OSWALD. Yes, do. And Regina shall stay as well. Regina shall be with me always. You will save me, Regina, won't you?

REGINA. I don't understand—

MRS. ALVING. Save you?

OSWALD. Yes—when the time comes.

MRS. ALVING. Oswald, you have your mother to save you!

OSWALD. You? [*Smiles.*] No, mother; that salvation you could never bring. [*Laughs sadly.*] You? Ha! [*He studies her.*] Although, who better to do it, if not you? [*Suddenly.*] Why must you always be so formal with me, Regina? Why can't you just call me Oswald?

REGINA. [*Softly.*] I don't think Mrs. Alving would like it.

MRS. ALVING. You'll soon have every right to. Now come and sit with us.

REGINA seats herself demurely and hesitantly at the other side of the table.

MRS. ALVING. And now, my poor, wretched boy, I am going to take the weight off your mind;—

OSWALD. Are you, mother?

MRS. ALVING.—all that terrible remorse and self-reproach you've told me of.

OSWALD. And you think you can do that?

MRS. ALVING. Yes, now I can, Oswald. A little while ago you spoke of the joy of life; and at that a new light burst over my life and everything in it.

OSWALD. I don't understand you.

MRS. ALVING. You ought to have known your father when he was a young lieutenant. He was overflowing with the joy of life!

OSWALD. Yes, I know.

MRS. ALVING. It was like a summer's day just to look at him. He was full of energy; full of hope!

OSWALD. Well—?

MRS. ALVING. Well… then this child of joy—for he was like a child in those days—had to set up home in a small, forgotten town which had no joys to offer him—only dissipations. He lacked any purpose to his life—he had only an official position; no work into which he could throw himself heart and soul—only business. And not a single friend who knew what it was to feel the joy of life—only idlers and drunks.

OSWALD. Mother—!

MRS. ALVING. So the inevitable happened.

OSWALD. The inevitable?

MRS. ALVING. You told me yourself, this evening, what would become of you if you stayed at home.

OSWALD. You mean to say that father—?

MRS. ALVING. Your poor father found no outlet for the overwhelming joy of life within him. And I brought no brightness into his home.

OSWALD. Not even you?

MRS. ALVING. I had been taught a great deal about duty and all the rest of it, all of which I went on obstinately believing in. Everything was marked out into duties—my duties, his duties—I am afraid I made this home intolerable for your poor father, Oswald.

OSWALD. Why have you never told me of this before?

MRS. ALVING. Until now I've never seen it as something I could share with you... you're his son.

OSWALD. What do you mean by that?

MRS. ALVING. [*Slowly.*] All I saw was that your father was a broken man since before you were born.

OSWALD. Ah—!

He rises and walks away to the window.

MRS. ALVING. And then; day after day, I dwelt on the fact that, by rights, Regina should also be at home in this house—just like my own boy.

OSWALD. Regina—!

REGINA. Me—?

MRS. ALVING. Yes, now you know.

OSWALD. Regina!

REGINA. So mother was that kind of woman.

MRS. ALVING. Your mother had many good qualities, Regina.

REGINA. Yes, but she was one of that sort all the same. Oh, I've often suspected it but— I should like to leave now madam, if I may.

MRS. ALVING. Are you sure, Regina?

REGINA. Yes.

MRS. ALVING. Well, you can do as you like, but –

OSWALD. Don't go! Your place is here.

REGINA. *Merci*, Mr. Alving—or now, I suppose, I may say Oswald. But I can tell you, this wasn't at all how I imagined it.

MRS. ALVING. Regina, I have not been frank with you—

REGINA. No, that you haven't. If I'd known that Oswald was an invalid, I would never have—Besides, now there can never be anything between us... No! I won't stay out here in the country just to wear myself out nursing sick people.

OSWALD. Not even one who's so near to you?

REGINA. I'm afraid not. A poor girl must make the best of her youth, or she'll be left out in the cold before she knows where she is. And I, too, have the joy of life in me, Mrs. Alving!

MRS. ALVING. Yes, unfortunately so. But don't throw yourself away, Regina.

REGINA. If that's what life has in store for me, then so be it; Oswald takes after his father; I suppose I must take after my mother.

A short pause.

May I ask, madam, if Pastor Manders knows my situation?

MRS. ALVING. Pastor Manders knows everything.

REGINA. Well then, I'd better see if I can still make the steamer. The Pastor's such a nice man to deal with, and I certainly think I've as much right to that money as that brute of a carpenter.

MRS. ALVING. You are very welcome to it, Regina.

REGINA. You might have brought me up as a gentleman's daughter, madam; it would have become me better. But never mind! [*With a glance at the unopened bottle.*] I may yet come to drink champagne with the great and the good.

MRS. ALVING. If you ever need a home, Regina, you shall always find one here.

REGINA. No, thank you, madam. I'm sure Pastor Manders will look after me. And if the worst comes to the worst, I know of one house where I'm sure to fit right in.

MRS. ALVING. Where's that?

REGINA. 'Chamberlain Alving's Home'.

MRS. ALVING. Regina, listen to me: that place will be your ruin!

REGINA. Oh, please! *Adieu.*

She nods and goes out through the hall.

OSWALD. Has she gone?

MRS. ALVING. Yes.

OSWALD. [*To himself.*] That was foolish.

MRS. ALVING goes up behind him and gently lays her hands on his shoulders.

MRS. ALVING. Oswald, my dear boy—has it shaken you very much?

OSWALD. All this about father, you mean?

MRS. ALVING. Yes, about your poor father. I hope it hasn't been too much for you.

OSWALD. Why should it? Of course it came as a great surprise; but it doesn't really make much difference to me.

MRS. ALVING. [*Drawing her hands away.*] Doesn't make much difference! That your father was so desperately unhappy?

OSWALD. Of course I pity him, I pity him as I would anyone else; but—

MRS. ALVING. But nothing more! Your own father!

OSWALD. [*Impatiently.*] Oh—'father', 'father'! I never knew anything of my father. I remember nothing about him, except that he once made me sick.

MRS. ALVING. But this is terrible! Shouldn't a son love his father, whatever happens?

OSWALD. When he has nothing to love his father for? has never known him, even? Do you really cling to that old myth?—you, who for the most part are so enlightened?

MRS. ALVING. Can it really be only a myth—?

OSWALD. Yes, of course it can! Surely you can see that, mother. It's one of the many dead ideas that are blindly accepted in the world, and so it is that—

MRS. ALVING. Ghosts!

OSWALD. Yes, why not? You might well call them that.

MRS. ALVING. [*Wildly.*] Oswald! Then you don't love me, either!

OSWALD. You I know, at least—

MRS. ALVING. Yes, you know me; but is that all?

OSWALD. And, of course, I know how much you love me, and I'm most grateful to you for that. And now that I'm ill you can be very useful to me.

A beat as MRS. ALVING contains the blow.

MRS. ALVING. Yes, I can, can't I, Oswald? Oh, I'm almost thankful for this illness now; that it's brought you home to me. For I can see that you're not mine yet: I shall have to earn your love.

OSWALD. [*Impatiently.*] Yes yes yes; that doesn't mean anything! Idle talk! You must remember I'm a sick man, mother. I don't have enough energy to think of other people; I have enough problems of my own to worry about.

MRS. ALVING. [*In a low voice.*] I shall be patient and easily satisfied.

OSWALD. And cheerful too, mother!

MRS. ALVING. Yes, my dear boy, you're quite right. [*Goes towards him.*] Now have I relieved you of all that remorse and self-reproach?

OSWALD. Yes, you have. But who will relieve me of the dread?

MRS. ALVING. The dread?

OSWALD. Regina might have done it.

MRS. ALVING. I don't understand you. What is this dread?—and why Regina?

OSWALD. Is it very late, mother?

MRS. ALVING. It's early morning.

She looks out through the conservatory.

The day is dawning over the hilltops. And the weather's clearing, Oswald. In a little while you shall see the sun.

OSWALD. I'm glad of that. Perhaps I will still have something to live for.

MRS. ALVING. Of course you will!

OSWALD. Even if I can't work—

MRS. ALVING. Oh, you'll soon be able to work again, my dear boy— now you've banished all those dark and depressing thoughts.

OSWALD. Yes, I'm glad you were able to rid me of those. And when I've finally got over this—

He sits on the sofa.

Now we must have a little talk, mother—

MRS. ALVING. Yes, let's.

She moves a chair over to the sofa, and sits down close to him.

OSWALD. And meanwhile the sun will be rising. And then you shall know everything. And I shall not feel this dread any longer.

MRS. ALVING. What is it I must know?

OSWALD. Mother, did you not say a little while ago that there was nothing in the world you would not do for me, if I asked?

MRS. ALVING. Yes, indeed I did.

OSWALD. And you'll stick to it, mother?

MRS. ALVING. You can rely on that, my dear boy; you're all I have.

OSWALD. Very well, then; I shall tell you—Mother, you're a wilful woman, I know. But please, sit quietly while I tell you this.

MRS. ALVING. You're going to tell me something dreadful.

OSWALD. You mustn't scream, do you hear? Promise me that. We shall sit and talk about it quietly. Do you promise me, mother?

MRS. ALVING. Yes, yes; I promise. Tell me!

OSWALD. Well then... You should know that all this fatigue—and my inability to think of work—all that is not the illness itself—

MRS. ALVING. Then what is the illness?

OSWALD. The disease I have as my birthright...

He points to his forehead and adds very softly:

—is seated here.

MRS. ALVING. Oswald! No—no!

OSWALD. Don't scream. I can't bear it. Yes, mother, it's here, waiting. And it may break out any day—at any moment.

MRS. ALVING. Oh! How awful!

OSWALD. That's enough!—that's enough! That's just the way things are now.

MRS. ALVING. [*Springing up.*] It's not true, Oswald! It's not possible; it can't be!

OSWALD. I've had one attack already. In Paris. It was soon over, but when I discovered the state I'd been in, then I felt the dread; so I came home to you as fast as I could.

MRS. ALVING. Then this is the dread—!

OSWALD. Yes—and of course it's so unspeakably awful. If only it had been an ordinary fatal disease—! For I'm not so afraid of death—though I should like to live as long as I can.

MRS. ALVING. Oh, yes, Oswald, you must!

OSWALD. But this is just so unbearably awful. To become like a helpless child again! To have to be fed! To have to—Oh! I can't even bring myself to say it!

MRS. ALVING. But a child will always have his mother to care for him.

OSWALD. [*Springing up.*] No, never! That I will not have. I can't stand to think that I might lie in that state for years and years—getting old and grey like that. And in the meantime you might die and leave me.

He sits again. This time in MRS. ALVING'S chair.

For the doctor said it wouldn't necessarily prove fatal at once. He called it a... a softening of the brain—something like that. [*Smiles sadly.*] I think that expression sounds so beautiful. It always makes me think of cherry-red velvet—something delicate and soft to the touch.

MRS. ALVING. [*Shrieks.*] Oswald!

OSWALD. [*Springing up again.*] And now you've taken Regina away from me. If only I could have had her! She would have saved me, I know she would have.

MRS. ALVING. [*Goes to him.*] What do you mean, my darling? There's no help in the world I would not give you!

OSWALD. When I recovered from my attack in Paris, the doctor told me that when it comes again—and it will come—there will be no more hope.

MRS. ALVING. He was heartless enough to—

OSWALD. I demanded it of him. I told him I had arrangements to make—[*He smiles cunningly.*] And so I had.

He takes a little box from his inner breast pocket and opens it.

Mother, do you see this?

MRS. ALVING. What is it?

OSWALD. Morphia.

MRS. ALVING. Oswald!—My boy!

OSWALD. I've manage to scrape together twelve capsules—

MRS. ALVING. Give me the box, Oswald.

OSWALD. Not yet, mother.

He hides the box again in his pocket.

MRS. ALVING. This will be the end of me!

OSWALD. No, mother, it will be the end of me. Now, if I had Regina here, I would tell her how things were—and beg her to save me. And she would have done it; I know she would.

MRS. ALVING. Never!

OSWALD. If she had seen me lying there helplessly, like an infant; hopeless and powerless and utterly lost—beyond all help—

MRS. ALVING. Regina wouldn't have done it. Not for all the world!

OSWALD. Regina would have done it; Regina was so splendidly free! She would soon have tired of nursing an invalid.

MRS. ALVING. Then thank God that Regina isn't here.

OSWALD. Well then, it's you who must save me, mother.

MRS. ALVING. [*Shrieks.*] I!

OSWALD. Who else?

MRS. ALVING. I'm your mother!

OSWALD. That's precisely why.

MRS. ALVING. It was I who gave you life!

OSWALD. I never asked you for life! And what sort of a life have you given me? I will not have it! You shall take it back again!

MRS. ALVING. Help! Help!

She runs out into the hall.

OSWALD. [*Going after her.*] Where are you going? Don't leave me!

MRS. ALVING. [*In the hall.*] To fetch the doctor, Oswald! Let me out!

OSWALD. [*Also outside.*] You're not leaving this house! And no one's coming in, either.

The locking of a door is heard. MRS. ALVING re-enters with OSWALD following.

MRS. ALVING. Oswald! Oswald—my child!

OSWALD. How can you love me if you allow me to suffer like this?

There is a moment's silence. MRS. ALVING steadies herself, nods slightly, looks at OSWALD and then extends her hand to him.

MRS. ALVING. Here's my hand.

OSWALD. Will you—?

MRS. ALVING. If it's ever necessary. But it won't be. No... No; it can't be!

OSWALD. Well, let us hope not.

He takes her hand.

And let us live together as long as we can.

He releases her hand.

Thank you, mother.

He seats himself in the arm-chair which MRS. ALVING has moved to the sofa. Day is breaking. The lamp is still burning on the table.

MRS. ALVING. Do you feel better?

OSWALD. Yes.

MRS. ALVING. [*Bending over him.*] It was all in your mind, Oswald—that's all. You've got yourself all worked up and it's all been too much for you. But now you'll have a proper rest at home with your mother. My dear, blessèd boy. Everything you want, you shall have, just like when you were a little child.—There now. It's all over. See how easily it passed! Oh, I knew it would.—And look, Oswald, what a beautiful day we're going to have! Brilliant sunshine! Now you shall really see your home, my son.

She goes to the table and puts out the lamp. Sunrise. The surface of the sea glows and shimmers in the morning light.

OSWALD sits in the arm-chair with his back towards the landscape. He doesn't move. Suddenly he says:

OSWALD. Mother, give me the sun.

MRS. ALVING. What did you say?

OSWALD. [*Repeats, in a dull, toneless voice.*] The sun. The sun.

MRS. ALVING. [*Goes to him.*] Oswald, what's the matter?

OSWALD seems to shrink into the chair; all his muscles relax; his face is expressionless, his eyes have a glassy stare.

MRS. ALVING. What's happening? [*Shrieks.*] Oswald! What's the matter with you?

She falls to her knees beside him and shakes him.

Oswald! Oswald! look at me! Don't you recognize me?

OSWALD. [*Tonelessly, as before.*] The sun.—The sun.

MRS. ALVING. [*Springs up in despair and shrieks.*] No! I can't bear it! I can't bear it! Never! [*Suddenly.*] Where are they?

She fumbles hastily in his breast pocket, looking for the box.

…where are they? There!

She finds the box, takes it, shrinks back a few steps and screams:

No! No! No!—Yes!—No! No!

She stands a few steps away from him with her hands twisted in her hair, and stares at him in speechless horror. OSWALD remains motionless.

OSWALD. The sun.—The sun.

FIN